Private Equity
&
Venture Capital

The ultimate guide to understand
the private equity world

By Killian Helf

For question or improvement: contact.khedition@gmail.com

ISBN: 9798845917720

About The Author

Killian Helf encourages his readers to make up their own stories. He uses his knowledge, but also the work of others (always sourced), to achieve his aim. To pique the reader's interest, he uses a plain writing style with tangible examples to assist the reader in seeing himself/herself in his discussions.

Killian Helf decided to resume his journey after acquiring a French cooking diploma and gaining some experience in the hospitality industry by quitting his job and enrolling in the Netherlands to study international finance and management. He is still in university and enjoys learning different topics in addition to his regular classes in order to expand his knowledge. This strategy is responsible for the publication of this book today. He developed a passion for the private equity business and all the mechanisms that surround it. By reading industry news and enrolling in several online classes. He has decided to publish this book as an icebreaker for all those who are interested in learning more about this fascinating subject.

Killian Helf's desire is to share the knowledge he has gained with those who are as eager to learn as he is.

Killian Helf is well-liked by his peers because he focuses on the most important topics and has a wonderful manner of passing on his knowledge through simple cases that adequately reflect the issue in question.

The author welcomes new comments and queries. Readers who are interested can contact him at the following email

address: contact.khedition@gmail.com

Dedication

For my grandma who always supported all my projects, my parents who gave me the possibility to become who I am and all my closest who helped me with this book.

Table of content

Introduction

The private equity world grows each year a little bit more and becomes a real alternative to the more well know ways of fundings a business. Of course, this industry has always existed but its democratization of it can be highlighted in this last decade. Many factors can explain that as the private equity funds which open their capital to retail investors, the transparency of startups on how to raise money, the different TV shows who develop on this topic, and so on.

However, for many people, this world stays dark, and lots of misunderstandings on this topic are made due to the myths and fake information that people may hear about private equity or simply due to the lack of education on this topic. But nowadays even more than before it is important to know how the economy works and omitting the private equity sector is hiding a part of the truth regarding it.

This book will provide general input about the private equity sector and allow to have a general idea of it, but for a purpose of understanding, it will not go in-depth for every subject and this book should be seen more as a first step in the private equity sector than an end in itself.

This book has been created for entrepreneurs but also for people willing to do a career in this field and who are looking to get a general idea of what is it really. This book focuses uniquely on the private equity itself, the mechanisms of the funds and the most common rules. However, the economic environment of the sector will not be developed. The goal was to enhance the work of a manager in a fund but in any case, to develop the general economy of the private equity.

Based on that the market of this sector will not be stated in this book, and I invite you to do further research about it if it is a topic that you are looking for.

To come back to the private equity world itself, all the people interesting in this sector may know Sequoia Capital, Andreessen Horowitz, and Accel which have financed the biggest companies in the world like Facebook, Apple, Spotify, Kayak, Deliveroo, Airbnb, Pinterest, and so many other companies which are now part of our daily life. However, this book will demonstrate that different types of investors can take place in this industry and that the type of structure will highly depend on the country in which the private equity fund has been set up and the goal of it, then the managerial process will be discovered where the step from raising money from a private equity point of view to invest this money and manage the company will be explained. Finally, the process of analyzing and evaluating a company will be explained to help any investor to have a realistic idea of the worth of his/her company but also understand how the private equity investor finds a price for it.

The last word before beginning, all the points developed in this book are backed by many articles, websites, books, papers, and videos to ensure the accuracy of the purpose. Nevertheless, feel free to get in touch with me if some points stay unclear or could be developed more to provide further input for future readers. The most useful sources used can be found at the end of the book.

Chapter 1:
A General Picture of
Private Equity

What is The Private Equity &Venture Capital?

First, before going further in this book, a definition of private equity must be established. This definition may be a little complicated since many things must be examined; nonetheless, it is based on three key features that everyone should consider when dealing with this topic.

On the one hand, private equity is a source of funding for a business. Private equity is a different manner of financing a business. This is a way as an IPO, bond issuance, or obtaining a loan from the banking system.

On the other hand, it is generally an investment made by a financial institution known as a private equity investor because the company is not listed on the stock exchange (The concept of a private equity investor will be explored further in Chapter 2).

The final point to consider when discussing the definition of private equity is the use of the term venture capital. Private equity is broad, and venture capital is a part of the possible private equity deal; it could be considered as a subset or sub-category. Indeed, venture capital is when a private equity investor invests in a firm still in its early stages of development or a startup.

However, the relationship between the private equity investor and the company backed by the private equity investor must be grasped. To illustrate this point, a concrete but basic example is needed.

Imagine a company needs money, and this firm wants to use private equity investment to raise money. To do so, the firm is going to issue new shares. These shares are bought by the private equity investor, and in exchange, the investor will give money to the company. However, the repercussions of this seemingly straightforward transaction based on the company and the private equity investor are significant.

The first result is that the private equity investor is not only a financier, like a bank that makes loans, but also a shareholder. The private equity investor can participate in business governance and support firm management.

The second implication is that the only way for a private equity investor to be compensated is through capital gain. And to make a gain, the investor needs to sell his/her shares higher than at the price he/she gets them.

As a result, practitioners frequently state that private equity investment is a marriage with an end because the company and the private equity must remain together, yet there is an end because the private equity must exit to earn the capital gain. So, when private equity investing is mentioned, these two storylines, being a financier and being a shareholder, always coexist.

But there is something else that needs to be understood, and the investor's perspective must be used to better understand the core process of a private equity transaction.

As stated previously, private equity is not the same as public equity, so to better understand the mechanisms of a private equity deal, it is preferable to compare it with a company list on the stock exchange to catch the main differences.

Three different characteristics need to be used to compare these two types of equity.

The first characteristic is regarding the liquidity of the company; if an investor is invested in a publicly traded company, liquidity is not an issue. If he/she wants to exit (by selling his/her shares), he/she presses the button, and the market provides liquidity. However, having liquidity as a private equity investor is difficult since he/she cannot use the stock exchange. He/She must find another investor willing to buy his/her shares. That means it could be time-consuming, complex, and sometimes challenging to gain liquidity through the private equity market.

The second characteristic concerns pricing or the value of his/her shares. If he/she owns shares in a company that is listed on a stock exchange, pricing is determined by the market. The pricing can be fair, unfair, cheap, or expensive, but pricing is not the issue. The stock exchange provides it. On the contrary, if he/she owns a private equity investment, the investor must always negotiate the share price with the other investors. And the negotiation can be more or less simple depending on the context.

The final characteristic is monitoring. As mentioned previously, the private equity investor is a shareholder in the company. It means that the private equity investor must safeguard his or her right to monitor the value generated by the investment. So, if the investor invests in a company listed on the stock exchange, his/her rights are governed by the stock exchange's statutes. And in several nations, there is highly relevant legislation that can safeguard minority stock owners as well. On the contrary, if he/she is a private equity investor, a contract about how the investor will safeguard his/her investment and the rights must be established.

These three main characteristics are always mentioned when private equity investing is mentioned. To be successful in this industry, an appropriate way to manage these three challenges must be found.

By Killian Helf

Why Companies Use Private Equity?

There are two distinct aspects of the private equity world. The financing part and equity investing part. In this section, a focus on the finance story will be made. To begin with this part, the main question should be asked: "why does a corporation need private equity to meet its financial needs?"

Accepting private equity on board for a firm is a difficult decision because it is not like a bank granting loans, where the bank delivers money to the company but remains an outsider. The private equity investor becomes an insider of the company, and the corporation must negotiate this "marriage." Both academia and practitioners frequently claim that a company accepts private equity for four important reasons, which can be seen as advantages.

The first advantage is the certification benefit. Suppose an entrepreneur accepts a private equity investor on board. In that case, he/she is, in a sense, certified because the private equity investor's decision to invest in a firm indicates that the company is of very high quality. As a result, the organization can use this stamp for advertising its attributes, profiles, and reputation throughout the industry. For example, if the entrepreneur wants to enter a new sector but he/she knows nothing about it, and the company's brand name is unknown, the entrepreneur might show that he/she has an excellent reputation because a private equity investor agreed to invest. At the same time, the company's brand is boosted thanks to the arrival of the investor.

The second advantage is the networking benefit. When a private equity investor invests in a company, he/she delivers strong support by providing access to his/her network, increasing prospects, and interacting with new suppliers and consumers. This is critical for a corporation looking to expand its sales.

The third advantage is the knowledge benefit. As a company shareholder, the private equity investor can transmit his or her knowledge to the company. For example, soft knowledge refers to the ability to manage a team, run a corporation, and deal with other players; nevertheless, knowledge might refer to something more complicated. For example, industrial understanding, chemical experience, and R&D competence; in this case, the knowledge will be named "hard knowledge." So, expertise is essential, especially for companies in their early stages of development, such as venture capital deals.

The final advantage is the financial benefit. This one is the most famous of all these fourth simply because a private equity firm invests in a company; the company obtains tremendous support. This support is provided by increasing the amount of equity and improving the company's credit status. That means the company's rating will rise, and as the company's rating increases, the company's ability to cut the cost of capital will be severely harmed.

investor is on board. However, the primary reason that requires the venue of a private equity investor in a company is the need for money.

But the reason why a firm requires funds is not always the same, and it is dependent on the stage of the company's life cycle; this concept is simple and gives an accurate idea of all the stages that a company will know during its life. Even if it is simple, the difference between each step of this cycle is to be grasped as this concept will be referred to several times in the coming chapters.

The reasons to raise capital are not the same and will highly depend on the stage where the company is located (beginning of life or end of life). It is what the cycle tries to highlight with these different phases. Further other life cycle models can be found online with a different number of steps (the most often between 3 and 7), but for the clarity of the purpose, the life cycle presented here will contain six main phases. The way to finance each phase will be explained because each step is more or less challenging for an entrepreneur who wants to finance his/her business due to, for instance, the risk. However, for each of these phases, some solutions to finance the activity are possible, and the most common solution would be provided to give a general picture of these possibilities.

The first stage of the company is when it requires funding to finance R&D activities throughout the first development phase. Concretely it is the creation of the business idea. This phase is difficult to finance because there is only an idea and nothing concrete; due to that, banks are unlikely to provide funds. In most cases, the investor at this phase is represented by the family, friends, the entrepreneur's savings, and in some instances, either a business angel or a private equity investor (which will be referred to as venture capital in this situation. However, this notion will be developed further in the book.

The second phase is the startup phase; funds are required to purchase fixed assets and finance working capital. During this phase, this risk is still high, and the most common investors would be the family, friends, and a business angel or a venture capital investor.

The third step is related to the early growth; the corporation requires additional capital to support the initial phase of expansion. The main player stays the venture capital investor when the company reaches this phase. However, the banking system can also offer funds when the first sales are made.

The fourth phase arrives when a firm is expanding, and its sales are increasing; it requires funds to purchase new fixed assets and finance working capital due to the rise in sales. During this phase, the banking systems and trade credit are likely to be the primary funding sources, but private equity may also be helpful in some cases.

The fifth phase could be represented as the mature age of the company; the corporation may require cash to acquire another company and manage new fixed assets. When the mature age is reached, the company can employ various choices. Some of these would be using a stock exchange by conducting an IPO, hiring a private equity investor, or using the banking system that is willing to help during this phase.

The sixth and final phase is the one of the declines; the company requires finances to try to flee the situation. This phase is the less liked phase by entrepreneurs who see the end of the story arriving. However, there are still some choices to finance the enterprise, hoping that thanks to these funds, the company will start again. But for the financing of this phase, there are many similarities with the first one, so the investors would be mainly family, friends, or a private equity investor specializing in this type of deal.

By Killian Helf

A Deeper View in the Cycle Life

The concept of a company's life cycle is crucial not just to comprehend why a company can use a private equity investor to satisfy a financial need but mainly because it will determine when to invest in private equity.

Thanks to the last part, a difference between private equity and public equity can be made. But the knowledge acquired regarding private equity is still broad. Practitioners say that it is an umbrella definition, implying that under it, a wide range of deals and activities can be discovered.

Better insights into the different private equity company deals can be found using the concept of a company's life cycle.

Development begins the life cycle; during this phase, the entrepreneur or researcher begins to create the business idea. Financially speaking, this phase is called "pre-seed funding," which refers to private equity investment in a firm during its early stages of development.

On to the second step, the company's startup, the entrepreneur flips the key to activate the business. In this situation, "startup financing or seed funding" refers to an investment made by a private equity investor who invests during the startup phase.

The third stage is the period of early growth. In this scenario, if a private equity investor meets the requirement for providing capital, the operation will be called "early growth financing." This is significant because "pre-seed," "startup," and "early growth financing" can be combined to form the venture capital cluster. Venture capital or VC is still part of the private equity but could be seen as a "sub-category".

During stage fourth, the company is in its expansion or growth phase, and its revenues are soaring. The investment of the private equity investor will be called "expansion financing."

Step five in private equity would be qualified as "replacement funding" this term is used when the company is in its mature age.

Then, if a private equity investor is investing in a company amid a crisis or downturn, the financial name of this phase would be "vulture financing."

These explanations allow realizing that even if there is one name and one definition of private equity, there are six separate businesses, six different indirect agreements, and six different markets, each with its concept of risk and reward for the investor. In each of the six markets, private equity might partner with a minority or a majority state; this will vary in function of the negotiation led.

Another notion that can be applied to all these six alternative clusters is that the private equity could take a hands-on or hands-off approach.

Hands-on indicates that the private equity firm provides extensive support to the company, not just in certification, networking, and so on; instead, the private equity firm works alongside the entrepreneur to lead and develop the company.

But the private equity firm's attitude and approach may be hands-off. This term indicates that the private equity firm provides extensive networking, certification, and understanding assistance, but the entrepreneur drives the car. Even if the Private equity firm offers a lot of assistance.

Venture Capital Activities

Now that the cycle life of a company has been properly defined, it is time to have a closer look at the six private equity deals possible. Firstly, the venture capital deals and then the other activities will be covered in the coming chapter.

The first step of venture capital is pre-seed funding. It is most likely the most sophisticated, risky, and challenging business for private equity investors. First and foremost, the definition of seed funding is straightforward. The funding of an R&D initiative aims to develop a patent that can be turned into a product as it is the funding of an R&D initiative. Not all the sectors are eligible for seed financing activities; the most common ones are often biological, chemical, information technology, and pharmaceutical. It makes sense to discuss seed financing in these areas. The goal of an R&D project is not to create a product but to create a patent, which may then be translated into a product. As it is possible to imagine, the risk is exceedingly significant in these situations. Because a research project to complete is needed, and once the project is found, a patent needs to be obtained. Even if the patent is delivered, it must be transformed into a product. To give an idea, market data state that in seed financing, three numbers must keep in mind (100, 10, and 1). To be a seed financier, the investor must screen one hundred projects, finance just ten, and only one will be successful. That demonstrates the extremely high amount of risk associated with an R&D project. As a result, private equity investors are sometimes unable to contribute not because the project is bad but because they already have too much risk associated with other investments of this type.

Then the second possible deal for venture capital is startup financing or seed financing. Again, the definition is straightforward. Startup finance provides funds to a firm that wishes to purchase fixed assets and working capital to turn the key and begin the entrepreneurial activity. The beginning is not the same as the seed. In this case, there is a business concept, a project, and a business strategy. The entrepreneur requires funds to begin his/her business. However, the risk remains extremely high because the private equity investor would rely on a business strategy, which can sometimes be very dangerous. As a result, private equity eager to participate in a company must negotiate in a complicated manner to safeguard his/her investment. For example, negotiating a put option is a popular approach to safeguarding a private equity investor. In case the business strategy or the business is not successful. A put option is to sell his/her shares to the entrepreneur and get his/her money back. The entrepreneur must have money; otherwise, having a put option in may be lovely, but it will not be profitable. If this concept still looks unclear, it will be developed more in-depth in chapter three.

The third possibility concerns early-stage financing. To use a practitioner's term, early growth financing is the financing of the day after. It does not imply money provided twenty-four hours after the company was created but rather a private equity engagement in the post-startup phase. When an entrepreneur starts a firm, he or she has a specific business plan. However, as the entrepreneurs start his/her activity, the environment changes dramatically, resulting in a financial gap. If the money needed to bridge the gap is not too large, the banking system may be willing to help. However, if the difference is significant, it will be difficult for the banking system to lend money. In this instance, an equity investment is required. But the function of the private equity investor is more than just providing capital. In this phase, the role of private equity is to have a hands-on approach to help the entrepreneur. In other words, the PEI assists the entrepreneur in rewriting the business strategy, analyzing the cause of the gap, and resuming firm operations.

These three processes just described are the ones that shape the venture capital sector. These three steps are among the riskiest, but they are also among the most profitable. However, as previously said, the risk must be assessed because only a small number of enterprises will reach maturity.

Expansion Financing

Now that the venture capital part has been covered, deal number four, expansion financing, can take place. When expansion financing is mentioned, it refers to the business's expansion phase. The notion of venture capital is left with evidence that a future successful firm is here, so it is not possible to consider it as an extremely young enterprise where its market would still be unknown.

Expansion financing is the financing of a company's growth process. Returning to the fundamentals of strategy, the development or growth of a corporation can be controlled in two ways.

The first strategy implies financing the expansion by internal or organic growth. That means the company grows on its own by merely investing in new fixed assets or announcing working capital. In this situation, the private equity investor's task is straightforward. The purpose of private equity is to provide funds to the firm to purchase fixed assets or finance working capital. The term "straightforward task" is used because the corporation has numerous options, such as using a mortgage, a credit line, or bonds, which are all very effective. A corporation chooses private equity for two reasons. The first reason is that private equity firm is eager to invest in the company; this means that money is relatively cheap in this scenario because the company may easily select the best offer from all the private equity firms. The second reason is that the corporation would prefer to use private equity to provide some benefits, such as knowledge or certification. In this situation, the company needs funds. Still, it requires much more to, for example, enter new markets, which creates the main difference with a bank that provides a loan as it would be unable to assist the company in entering a new market.

However, the second strategy is based on external growth. This is much more complicated because external expansion implies that the company wishes to acquire another company, which impacts increasing sales significantly. When external growth is stated, in numerous cases, it is because the company decides to join a new market or entirely other business fields. In this case, the function of the private equity investor is different. In external growth (also called Merger & Acquisition or M&A), the company wishes to buy another company to expand sales. In this situation, the function, or role of private equity, is much more complex because private equity is not simply a provider of funds to buy the other company; instead, private equity is an advisor and consultant to the company. In this case, its approach could qualify as very hands-on.

The first task of a private equity investor is to assist the firm in scouting the market and identifying the company's name that makes sense to acquire. This is quite common. For example, currently, many European corporations want to buy another company in India, China, Indonesia, or Brazil. Still, they do not know the company's name that makes sense to buy. The role of the private equity during this first phase would be to scout the market and find a suitable company for an M&A.

The second task of private equity is to begin negotiating with possible targets to determine whether it makes sense to undertake an M&A.

The third function of private equity is providing funds to a company to acquire another. In this instance, two options are possible. The first is that the private equity investor lends money to the firm, receives shares from the company, and has enough money to complete the M&A. If the merger and acquisition are successful, the company and the target will merge. The second alternative is when the private equity investor establishes an SPV (stands for special purpose vehicle). Concretely, this SPV is a new company, an empty shell in which the private equity investor will deposit money with equity and the firm; together, they will collect money from the banking system, and the SPV will have enough cash to buy the other company. In the market, the option of creating an SPV is usually used for two reasons:

The first reason is that an M&A requires a substantial amount of debt, and the corporation does not want to raise the debt on its balance sheet.

The second reason is related to the fact that by employing the SPV, it is possible to retain the firm's characteristics, profile, and value entirely separate from the value of the acquisition. This is especially significant when the company does not want the private equity investor to profit from the merger's conclusion.

The final step in the M&A process, which is again driven by private equity, is to provide legal and tax help to run the acquisition and coordinate the merger.

So, two distinct approaches where one is more a hands-off approach while the second is a definitively hand-on approach. Nothing is predetermined, and this decision must be taken depending on the need of the company which wants to buy another one. However, a private equity investor with a hands-on approach is more common for an M&A deal as lots of responsibility is involved and a certain amount of knowledge is required to carry out the deal.

By Killian Helf

Replacement Financing

Replacement financing is the fifth private equity transaction possible and remember that it is the financing for a mature company. This definition, however, does not help much. To have a better understanding, a look at what is hidden underneath this term would be helpful.

The term "replacement" can help to understand the private equity investor's role during this phase. Concretely replacement financing is the action of replacing a current stakeholder with another one. Even if it is straightforward, two nuances should be carried in this mechanism.

The first nuance is that replacement funding is broad, while there is proof of three different deals to investigate behind this description.

The first possible deal is private equity buyouts which are increasingly popular, particularly in the United States and the United Kingdom. By adding these two markets, buyouts account for roughly 40 to 45 percent of the private equity market.

Buyouts are private equity transactions based on a particular technicality. The job of private equity in a buyout is not to finance a company.

But to discover viable targets for 100% acquisition.

An SPV is established when a private equity firm identifies a possible acquisition target. In the last part, when the explanation has been made, it has been stated that an SPV is an empty shell into which the private equity investor invests and becomes the sole shareholder. However, some other details can be added. Throughout this SPV, the private equity raises a lot of money to pay off obligations, and the usual debt-to-equity ratio is between 80 and 90 percent. That suggests the SPV makes extensive use of debt. This leverage allows the private equity investor to acquire a large sum of money by utilizing loans and equity. After that, all the funds are in the SPV, and it can buy another company with this money. And the acquisition could be a purchase or a negotiation. It could also be particularly aggressive as a hostile takeover that takes place through a stock exchange public bid.

At the end of the procedure, the SPV acquires ownership of the target. That means the private equity investor becomes the target's sole owner. The only result of this approach is that the firm acquired by private equity obtains all the SPV's debt on its balance sheet. Following the acquisition, the private equity investor's goal is not to run the firm but to hold it in the portfolio for a limited period before selling it to another buyer. This time is called the selling process, and it is simple because the private equity investor has the option of selling the entire company. These types of transactions could be positive or terrible; it mainly depends on how the negotiation has been led or the initial intention of the private equity investor.

The second deal is represented by PIPE. PIPE is an acronym that stands for private investment in public equity. In this situation, the DNA of the private equity deal is altered as it is for a buyout.

Once again, the corporation does not need money at the story's start. The scenario begins with a private equity firm eager to manage an investment. In this case, the private equity investor is a minority stakeholder in a public traded corporation. That is odd since, as in the first paragraphs of this book, it has been stated that private equity is not the same as public equity, and this time, the private equity investor will invest in a publicly traded company. Indeed, it is not. Because the private equity investor's goal is to take advantage by buying shares and selling them to another buyer at a price unrelated to the stock exchange, it works in such a way that the private equity investor can purchase a minority stake with the expectation that this number of shares will be sufficient to determine who will own the company. If an investor has enough shares to decide who will be the owner of a particular company, negotiating pricing is not a problem. These offers are becoming increasingly common in the United States, but notably in Europe, where banks represent the targets, and private equity investors will invest in publicly traded banks.

The third and final deal possible is the corporate governance deal. In this case, the DNA of private equity is altered because, unlike in the previous two, the story's beginning is not tied to the company's need for funds.

The fact that the corporation needs to rebuild its corporate governance represents the story's beginning. For example, consider a family business succession. In this situation, the function of private equity is to purchase certain shares from an existing shareholder to become an insider of the company and work as an insider to overhaul the company's corporate governance completely. If the private equity firm does an excellent job, it can sell the shares to the company's new shareholders. These transactions are now increasingly typical in nations where the family business is particularly prominent, such as Italy, Spain, and Germany.

The second nuance is related to the first; as seen in these three possible deals, the DNA of private equity is slightly altered. The DNA of private equity is predicated on the idea that the company needs money, and that private equity will finance it. This criterion is modified in the case of replacement finance as the primary goal in this step is no longer to raise funds for the company's own business but mainly to invest in other companies (to acquire them).

Vulture Financing

Vulture financing is the sixth and last private equity transaction. It is the financing of a declining company, and the private equity investor will finance the final stage of the company's life cycle. This label, like in replacement funding, is broad, and there is evidence of two different deals inside it. The reason is that a company's crisis status can be regulated in two different ways.

The first type of deal is restructuring financing. The concept is that a corporation is in crisis yet still alive. That means the company needs money to pay the other financiers or suppliers and invest in new fixed assets to relaunch the business or devise a new strategy. That implies the organization requires more than just money; it also requires extensive strategic help. If a private equity investor wishes to invest in this type of transaction, it must play two roles a financer on the one hand and a consultant and advisor to the company on the other. It is more or less what happens in the early growth financing where private equity has to support the company; in this case, PEI has to help the company a lot.

However, modifying the transaction at this moment is highly dangerous because the private equity investor is investing in a firm that is in crisis, and redesigning the strategy could be challenging. As a result, restructuring agreements are uncommon in private equity, and if a private equity investor is prepared to invest, he/she usually wants to be the majority shareholder. The reason is that private equity firms desire the ability to change management, replace the CEO, and radically rethink the business. It is a tricky business that makes the deal and the business harder.

The second type of deal is distressed financing. It refers to the funding of a bankrupt corporation, and that is a financing of a non-existent corporation. It appears to be a contradiction because if a firm default, the corporation cannot get money.

Due to that, the word financing is only used to have the same terminology as the other deals. However, a distressed financing transaction is one in which a private equity investor purchases assets from a failed corporation. For example, it could be a brand name, patents, and high-quality equipment and machinery. The corporation has defaulted in each of these examples, and the private equity investor wishes to acquire these assets. Private equity's desire to acquire these properties is tied to two distinct storylines.

The first one is that the private equity investor is a "dealer of assets," which means that the private equity acquires assets and sells them to others.

The second one is that the private equity investor purchases these assets and reinvests them in other companies in his or her portfolio to boost their worth.

Purchasing assets from a bankrupt company is complex since private equity must negotiate the purchase with the court. Because rules differ from country to country, the court controls the process of defaulting in all countries. And the bargaining could be difficult because the court's goal is to maximize the amount of cash available to meet the needs of suppliers, banks, and so on. So, it is a complex negotiation, and in many situations, the court wants to give the private equity investor some poison pills. Poison pills are symbolized, for example, by certain mortgages or the fact that a private equity investor wants to buy a plant or machinery. Still, there are a lot of workers inside the plant or machinery, and it is very tough to negotiate with them.

Unfortunately, or luckily, depending on the point of view, distressed finance is a highly popular deal in nations where the GDP is not high or where there are a lot of defaults, such as Europe, where these agreements are prevalent.

Finally, how these transactions are carried out is directly tied to the quality of the law. For example, in the United States, where the rules of distress finance are straightforward and relatively simple, these types of transactions function extremely effectively.

Chapter 2:

Private Equity In The Different Regions Of The Globe

General Idea of Private Equity Investors

It is now the time to understand the private equity industry and why a corporation would employ private equity.

Understanding that requires exploring the world of private equity investors and learning about who they are and how they operate. Because in chapter one, it has been stated that private equity investors are financial organizations that do just that. But now, it is time to figure out their qualities and how they are governed. The task is not simple because the world is vast, and plenty of regulations must be considered. It may become quite tough to choose one country over another. But in private equity, fortunately, there is evidence of two different models regulating private equity investments worldwide.

On the one side, the European Union model is governed by European Union directives. On the other side, there is the Anglo-Saxon model, which is governed by the laws of the United States and the United Kingdom, where private equity originated. Even if these two models have names of a region in the world, these can be applied way broader; for instance, Brazil, Turkey & Russia use the European Union model, while India, Australia, and commonwealth countries use the Anglo-Saxon one. In addition, as these two models are used worldwide, they help streamline the job of a private equity investor or entrepreneur in a certain way.

Firstly, the European Union format should be generally explained. To understand the regulation of private equity within the European Union, two significant directives that govern the entire financial system have to be developed because the ideology in Europe is that private equity is a financial service. As a result, it is governed by the directive that regulates the entire financial system.

In Europe, only two directives govern the financial system: the banking directive and the financial services directive. The main idea behind the two directives is that the financial system must be organized with a proper balance of efficiency and stability; while the other fundamental rule is that any financial institution which begins to operate in the financial system must be approved by a local supervisor or, in the case of banks, by the European Central Bank. After approval, financial institutions can market their services. They are monitored by local supervisors such as the Bank of Italy, the Bank of France, the Bundesbank, or the European Central Bank in the case of banks. When it comes to private equity, three different companies can be private equity investors. Remember that only these three entities can invest in private equity or function as private equity investors. The three distinct legal entities are Banks because banks are ubiquitous and may provide: any service in Europe, closed-End Funds for private equity investors and Investment firms.

The principles are radically different when looking at the Anglo-Saxon format, which is mainly used in the United States and the United Kingdom. Under this model, private equity is not a financial service but an entrepreneurial activity similar to managing any firm. This is not to say that the financial system is not involved. To understand how private equity works, a mix of common law in the United States and the United Kingdom, ad hoc fiscal regulations, and unique laws enacted to manage the private equity system must be examined. Another point to clarify is that in the Anglo-Saxon structure, there is no supervisory authority as there is in the European Union. These two distinct formats are crucial for comprehending the operation of the global private equity sector.

The presence of two formats is less critical for a local player. For example, suppose the PEI is Italian, French, or German acting locally. In that case, he/she just needs to use the European Union format, as if the PEI is a US private equity investor looking to invest in the US. On the contrary, if the investor is a global player operating in multiple countries, having two different formats is critical since he/she may wish to employ a European Union format in some circumstances and a US/UK format in others. Legal entity knowledge is more than just a legal issue; it is also a business issue in private equity investments.

Overview of the Closed End Funds

In the first part of this chapter, two legal formats (the European Union and the Anglo-Saxon) have been presented and explained in what both shape the world of private equity. It is now time to investigate the methods of private equity inside the framework of the European Union.

As previously stated, the European Union has three vehicles: banks, closed-end funds, and investment firms.

The first factor that needs to be explained is the Closed-end funds which are governed by the financial services directive, as well as the new AIFM (Alternative Investment Fund Managers Directive) regulation which aims to improve the quality of closed-end funds in the European Union. Closed-end funds are the most important vehicle for acting as a private equity investor in Europe. They are essential to understanding the mechanism of private equity investment in Europe and globally.

To comprehend closed-end funds, the three actors who made them up must be understood. These three actors are engaging with one another.

The first factor is the AMC (asset management company) which is a financial entity that has been approved and overseen by local supervisors, such as the Bank of Italy, the Bank of France, the Bundesbank, or other local supervisors in the European Union, and whose role it is to manage a fund or investor money. The AMC is comparable to a consulting firm in that it is not a financial organization directly investing cash but rather a group of professionals advising investors and managing their money. The European Union does not impose any restrictions on the shareholders of an AMC, so shareholders of an AMC could be any player, even though there is evidence in the market of three distinct, in a sense, families of AMCs: AMCs owned by banks; AMCs owned by private individuals, known as boutiques of private equity; and AMCs owned by states. The final factor is related to the fact that an AMC does not invest money, but every time an AMC launches a fund, which means it begins managing the money of other investors, the AMC is required to invest at least 2% of the fund's value. This is critical for generating a sense of commitment between the asset management firm and the size of the fund itself.

The second factor is associated with the closed-end fund itself. To understand what a closed-end fund is, it is necessary to understand what a fund is. A fund is just a common pool, or a bank account, into which investors can deposit their money. Investors automatically lose any entitlement to tailor-made management of their money when they place their money into a fund. They decide to do so because by pooling all the money, they can profit from greater diversification from the common pool and higher economies of scale from the fact that there is a lot of money coming from multiple investors. When an investor puts his or her money in the fund, he or she receives a certificate representing the amount invested.

Funds can be either open-ended or closed-ended. Funds are open-ended in the sense that investors can enter and exit the fund at any time and are closed end when investors can only invest at the start and exit only at the end. Private equity is managed through closed-end funds. Because investors can only invest in the beginning and exit at the end, the asset management company, thanks to that, is under no pressure to manage liquidity. As mentioned in chapter one, liquidity is a problem in private equity as it is difficult for the fund to exit from private equity investments without losing substantial gain.

Investors constitute the third player involved in these deals. Investors are those who put their money into a fund because they believe in the asset management company's abilities. Who exactly are investors? There are no legal limits, but empirical evidence suggests that common investors in closed-end funds are high-net-worth people, banks, insurance firms, pension funds, corporations, and/or states. More generally, it means large investors are willing to take on a high-risk, sophisticated venture like private equity.

The process of closed-end fund investing in private equity is represented throughout these three actors: AMC, closed-end funds, and investors. A fundamental guideline is that a closed-end fund can only invest the money received from investors. In that instance, a closed-end fund cannot legally raise funds through debt, and this means that the closed-end fund's investments cannot be leveraged.

A closed-end fund's operation is not simple. Previously stated that a closed-end fund is one in which investors put their money in at the beginning of the fund and exit only at the end, allowing the asset management company adequate time to engage in any liquid investment, such as private equity. However, the story is far more complex and is governed by a document known as the Internal Code of Activity. And this document is a set of rules established by the supervisor that govern how the closed-end fund operates.

To understand how a closed-end fund works, it is helpful to distinguish the many elements that make up a fund's life cycle in terms of timing. The fund research does not begin at the beginning of the fund. This may come as a surprise, but the commencement of a closed-end fund occurs before time zero, which has a maximum duration of one and a half years. This is known as fundraising. The asset management company has up to one and a half years to convince investors to invest in the closed-end fund. The legislation says nothing about the fund size, but the average size of a closed-end fund in Europe ranges between 100 and 300 million Euros.

Another consideration is that each investor's investment, named "one ticket," is usually priced at one million euros. For instance, if a fund wants to raise 100 million euros for a closed-end fund, it must persuade 100 investors to contribute one million euros. In some cases, each investor can buy more than one ticket, which will raise money from fewer investors. For instance, if each investor buys 20 tickets at 1 million, the fund will need only five investors to finance it.

However, fundraising is challenging. Fifty percent of all the fundraising in Europe failed to achieve its goals due to logistical challenges. It is especially difficult for impoverished, young, and less well-known asset management firms to persuade investors to invest their money.

If the asset management company receives the total amount, the fundraising process is completed, and the closed-end fund activities can begin. But investors do not have to provide the fund with the entire amount at the start. This is a wise option because the asset management firm cannot invest such a large sum of money all at once at time zero. After all, as it is a private equity, the asset management firm requires time. As a result, the asset management business has the authority to use a maximum of three years. These three years are known as a draw-down period. The draw-down period is when the asset management business can seek investors for a percentage of their commitment. For example, suppose a closed-end fund is launched, and the asset management company says, "Dear investor, give me 10% of your commitment." And typically, investors give the AMC 10% of their pledge in ten working days. After year three, the entire sum must be transferred to the closed-end fund. The asset management company is free to navigate and seek new assets, manage investments, and, most importantly, exit to create a capital gain.

Finally, the closed-end fund is coming to an end. Again, the legislation says nothing, but the typical lifespan of a closed-end fund in Europe is ten years. That means when the end of the ten years is reached; the AMC will have a choice to continue or not for three more years. It can be an interesting option because private equity is not a liquid investment. In year ten, the closed-end fund may lack liquidity because most of the private equity assets remain in place. As a result, the AMC may be able to take three more years, and the AMC can use the remaining three years to exit the various investments. When the thirteen years is reached, or perhaps sooner, the closed-end fund must cease operations. That means the AMC will have to meet with the investors, determine how much money is in the closed-end fund, and distribute the money among them in proportion to the number of tickets they purchased at the start of the fundraising.

The final factor that must be grasped to fully comprehend closed-end funds is the concept of profit mechanisms. That implies that the principle of how the AMC and the investors will profit must be figured out. Some information is already known as the fact that investors will receive money towards the conclusion of the fund, which might be year 10 or year 13, depending on the longevity of the fund, but based on this information; it is possible to dig into the principle to have a better understanding.

An internal code of activity governs profit mechanisms. For each internal code of activity for each closed-end fund, procedures will be provided to determine profit for both the AMC and the investors. AMC will receive two sorts of profit or revenue based on the best practices in the industry, and management fees and carried interest are the two sorts of revenues. These two designations are critical for closed-end funds and any private equity vehicle worldwide.

The management fee is the amount of money the AMC company receives each year from the closed-end fund. Concretely the closed-end fund is the vehicle that generates revenues and costs because, in a closed-end fund, there are capital gains generated by the exit of investment and losses if the exit is not successful. The AMC deducts a management fee from the closed-end fund's assets every year. The management fee is a predetermined percentage of the fund's initial monthly value. For example, if a closed-end fund has 100 million euros and the management fee is 2%, the AMC will earn two million Euros yearly from the closed-end fund. Obviously, with the management fee, the AMC must labor and incur significant expenses. Because the AMC must pay the management and confront operating costs, it also has to listen to the advice of the corporations that help the AMC execute its work. In addition, the AMC must pay the so-called technical committee. It is a committee of wise individuals who support the AMC managers doing their work. Thus there are a lot of charges. It is critical to establish who owns the AMC since if the AMC belongs to a bank or a large financial group, facing these expenses is not a problem. It may be difficult if the AMC is an independent private equity boutique.

The second way to generate revenue is based on the carried interest, which is also the most used way for this purpose. Carried interest can even be seen as a goal or a desire for an AMC as it will make its revenue. A closed-end fund's carried interest is calculated only at the end of its life. The carried interest mechanism is straightforward. It is a fixed percentage that the AMC will receive based on the difference between the ultimate IRR of the funds and a hurdle rate that was negotiated at the outset. For example, if the fund set up the carried interest at 30%;(which is a standard as the range is between 25 to 30%). The hurdle rate at8% (which is also a standard because hurdle rates range between 7 and 8%). The AMC will receive the carried interest only if the fund's final IRR is greater than 8%. In the case of a higher IRR, the AMC will be paid 30% of the difference between the final IRR and the hurdle rate.

This formula of carried interest is sometimes referred to as a waterfall mechanism, and it is worth noting that waterfall mechanisms can be used with or without catch-up. If the carried interest is based on the difference between the final IRR and the hurdle rate, it is called without catch-up. If the present interest is calculated immediately on the total amount of the final IRR, it is called catch-up. The carried interest is essential for calculating the amount of money the AMC will receive. As a result, at the end of the closed-end fund, investors will get the fund's principal amount less the AMC's carried interest.

Every important part regarding the closed-end funds has been covered. At the same time, the mechanism of private equity had shown that it is far more complicated than what was stated at the beginning of the book when it was mentioned that a private equity investor is simply a financial institution that invests in companies that are not publicly traded. This scenario is even more complex since investors put their money into a fund managed by an asset management business. Investors put their money in because they trust the asset management company's ability to manage private equity investments.

Banks & Investment Firms

While closed-end funds are the most common vehicle in Europe, they are not the only vehicle or legal organization that may be used to qualify as a private equity investor. In Europe, there are also banks and investment firms.

Banks are permitted to participate directly in private equity since banks in Europe are universal, which means they can invest in any financial asset. However, it is unusual for a bank to participate directly in private equity. The traditional approach for a bank to be active in the private equity industry is to have an AMC or invest in a closed-end fund. And if a bank owns an AMC, it does so because it wants to profit from the carried interest, but a bank invests in a closed-end fund because it wants to benefit from the capital gain at the end. But it is essential to understand why a bank rarely invests directly in private equity; there are two main reasons.

The first is that when banks invest to calculate regulatory capital in accordance with Basel II and Basel III requirements, the amount of regulatory capital is relatively large. Due to this important amount, even if the bank creates capital gain, most of this capital gain is neutralized by the cost of regulatory capital the bank must calculate.

The second reason is that banks investing directly in private equity must adhere to a slew of legal restrictions that make owning a significant percentage of a firm directly controlled by the same bank which invests; this situation creates a complex one as it is less interesting for the investors.

However, a bank may invest directly in private equity, especially if it wants to invest in a trophy firm (a very relevant company, where a bank may invest directly to save the company because it is appropriate for a specific area or account).

But in fact, the direct investment in private equity from the bank is negligible due to the regulation and the attractivity of the bank to do that.

Investment firms represent the other legal entity. According to the banking directive, investment businesses are financial institutions. They can perform the same functions as banks, except being able to accept deposits. As a result, investment firms can make direct investments in private equity. The mechanism of an investment firm is straightforward. On the liability side, there is shareholder equity and obligations. On the asset side, capital is accumulated through loans and equity, which can be invested in private equity. However, two types of people are required in private equity. On the one hand, there is a need to have individuals to manage like an AMC and people who are willing to invest like a closed-end fund. Two groups of shareholders are needed to reproduce this notion in an investing firm.

A-shareholders are shareholders who manage the investment firm and do the same function as an AMC. At the same time, B-shareholders are shareholders who cannot control a company but invest like investors in a closed-end fund. In terms of remuneration, A-shareholders will receive a management fee each year and a carried interest because the investment firm is not a fund with an end date but rather a financial institution. The carried interest must be calculated every year. The difference between the profit and the carried interest paid to A-shareholders will be distributed to B-shareholders.

Finally, it is important to emphasize that two distinct types of investors employ investment firms. On the one hand, investors that wish to leverage will hire investment firms since an investment business can do so and remember that closed-end funds cannot use leverage. The other group of investors is often a small number of investors who want to construct their captive vehicle and hence do not want the regulatory restraints that come with a closed-end fund but merely want to create their vehicle to invest their money in private equity. This is widespread, and there are many examples of family offices all around Europe. This refers to investment enterprises formed by two or three family members who want to invest and manage their own money directly.

Limited Partnerships In The US

It is time to enter the Anglo-Saxon system, which involves learning about the other format utilized worldwide to manage private equity investors. As previously stated, the Anglo-Saxon framework is associated with the United States and the United Kingdom. The United States would be explained first because it is the world's largest market for private equity.

The US market must be approached differently than the European one. In Europe, it begins with two significant directives governing financial systems. While in the United States, the ad hoc norms, special laws, and tax structure that govern private equity investment must be examined. When all these components are combined, it results in five different vehicles running private equity investments in the United States.

The venture capital fund is the first type of vehicle able to run private equity investors. Venture capital funds, also called VCFs, are the most common vehicle in the US. It is important to note that the term "fund" used in the US is a bit different than when it is used in Europe, and the reason will be developed later in this part.

Now that the foreword has been mentioned, it is possible to investigate about Venture Capital Fund. As stated, it is the most suitable vehicle for private equity and the world's largest private equity market. A venture capital fund is merely a definition, not a legal organization. The limited partnership, or simply the LP, is the legal entity. A limited partnership must be defined; it is a legal structure in the United States that is distinguished by the presence of two distinct groups of shareholders. Limited partners and general partners. Limited partners must have 99 percent of the shares, whereas general partners must hold 1 percent. Limited partners, or

LPs, are pure investors, meaning they do not manage the venture capital fund and are only accountable for a limited amount of money. Limited liability means that the worst-case scenario for them would be to lose all their money. General partners, or simply GPs, must manage the vehicle and are not merely investors. They are the managers, and they bear complete responsibility on an individual basis, so they are entirely responsible. This presence of LPs and GPs is ideal for private equity investments because, as in closed-end funds, there are two different groups of people.

The people who manage, which is the AMC, and the people investing, which are the investors. In a venture capital fund, it is the same legal entity because LPs are investors, and GPs are the managers. The distinction between the US and Europe is that GPs can only invest 1%, whereas, in Europe, the AMC must invest 2% of the fund's value. US regulation is highly relevant because if a limited partnership invests only in private equity and has a ten-year maturity, the vehicle is tax transparent. That means the legal entity (in this case, the limited partnership) does not pay taxes.

Finally, to complete the image, LPs and GPs must govern their relationship or existence together. While in Europe, there is an internal code of conduct that governs the relationship between investors and management, in the United States, because there is no supervisor, LPs and GPs must establish a contract. And the contract is known as the LPA (Limited Partnership Agreement). This LPA covers all the private equity rules that can be imagined when investing in the private equity market, for example, the size of the vehicle, the class in which they intend to invest, the amount of the management fee, and the amount of the carried interest. General partners, or those in charge of the business, will be paid a management fee in the same way that the AMC is paid in Europe and a carried interest calculated in the same way.

So, while the legal entities differ greatly between the United States and Europe, the foundation of the business remains the same. Finally, the definition of being entirely liable differs greatly between the United States and Europe. General partners want to protect themselves because they are liable. The remedy, popular in the United States, is for general partners to form an LLP. They function as limited partners in an LLP, which is a limited liability partnership. In this scenario, the LLP is the fully accountable LLP and represents the managing firm. That is, if the limited partnership wishes to collect a debt and completely discontinue the method now in place in the United States, the LLP must have the guarantee that collateral has been appropriated to acquire funding from the banking system.

In conclusion, leverage makes LPs very similar to investment firms but very distinct from closed-end funds, which, as mentioned previously, cannot leverage.

SBIC in the US

Even if venture capital funds are the most crucial vehicle in the US market, it is essential to examine the other possibilities to have a complete picture of the market. The second one in the US market is the SBICs. The SBIC (small business investment companies) were established by an act passed in 1958, the SBIC Act, which is widely regarded as a watershed moment in the history of US private equity. The US government established SBICs in 1958 to encourage the private equity market, particularly the venture capital industry. SBIC research was so successful that SBICs are now regarded as the ideal example of a PPP strategy to promote venture capital. PPP stands for public-private partnership. Many governments and policymakers in Europe and Asia are debating whether it makes sense to introduce this type of vehicle in their own countries.

Now that the general context has been explained, a more concrete explanation of an SBIC should be provided. An SBIC is a vehicle in which there are only two shareholders. One of the two shareholders must be a US public administrator (a state, such as California, or a municipality, such as New York City) and own 50 percent of the company. The other 50% shareholder can be any investor. A private investor is usually a bank, a corporation, or a private individual. These two shareholders' obligations and privileges are fundamentally different. That is intriguing because the government is simply a pure investor. This means that the US public administration cannot administer the vehicle. However, the other shareholder must. Given the economic link, it is interesting that both shareholders would receive a management fee to justify their participation.

Still, profit distribution is asymmetric in the event of profit computed using the current interest rate. Asymmetric means that the US government will receive funds up to a particular point specified in the SBIC agreement, with the additional profit going to the other investor. The SBIC allows a private investor to form a joint venture with a public administration, but the private investor has the option to run the vehicle and profit more than 50% of the share. Losses are evenly allocated 50 percent and 50 percent. Another interesting element is that the vehicle can leverage like venture capital funds, which means there is more money to be invested, and 33 percent of the leverage is guaranteed by the Federal Reserve of the United States at an exceptional price. This means that this entity can raise funds in debt at a very cheap interest rate. This perfectly illustrates how the combination of these features and the fact that this vehicle does not pay taxes is a fantastic approach to promoting venture capital and private equity in a system.

Banks, Corporate Venture & Business Angels

The two main vehicles have been explained. However, there are still three others that may be interesting to develop, even if there are less meaningful.

Regarding the Banks, it is the same features as exhibited in Europe. That means banks are only marginally interested in direct investment for the same reasons examined in Europe. Banks often operate as limited or general partners in a venture capital fund. That is why Banks will not be developed further, and the focus would be made only on the other two stories, which are far more interesting to examine.

The other two situations are equally striking. A corporate venture is yet another unique American story. A corporation is not a legal entity. A corporate venture is a corporation division whose sole purpose is to manage venture capital investments, primarily seed, and startup investments. However, unlike venture capital funds, the goal of a corporate venture is not to produce IRR, which means management fees and covered interest, but rather to generate good projects that can be employed by the business itself to improve the level of the corporation's value.

Finally, there are business angels. They are active in the United States, particularly in venture capital, seed financing, and startup finance. Business angels are governed by the law in the United States because they can be high-net-worth people, charities, or foundations, and they receive a specific benefit known as the QSBS rule, which stands for Qualified Small Business Stocks. The notion is that if a business angel invests in the equity of a small business that is not listed on the stock exchange and then exits if the capital gain is reinvested in another equity of QSBS, the business angel does not pay taxes. This is a fantastic incentive to promote the private equity sector and double the energy and money that a business angel is willing to support in the US venture capital system. As a result, this law is seen as a model to be imitated worldwide.

Funds & VCTs in the UK

The other side of the Anglo-Saxon system is represented by the UK market, which, along with the US, is truly the birthplace of private equity. As in the United States, the United Kingdom does not have, as does Europe, laws governing the entire financial system that assist in identifying features of private equity investors. Private equity in the United Kingdom, like in the United States, is governed by a patchwork of ad hoc rules and tax regulations. In the UK, as in the US, there is evidence of five alternative solutions for acting as a private investor. Venture capital funds, venture capital trusts, banks, business angels, and local PPPs are the five solutions (public-private partnerships). Some of the information has already been covered, and this is for two reasons.

The first one is that because the US and the UK have common law, venture capital funds are the same as in the US. The second reason is that tax regulations in the US and the UK wish to keep, in a sense, the same conditions for both players. That means that, worldwide, investors are free to choose the US or the UK to establish their venture capital fund based on strategic or geographical difficulties.

The most important vehicle in the UK, as in the US, is limited partnership venture capital funds. It is a vehicle that can act as a private equity investor by leveraging a lot, which multiplies the amount of money that can be invested in private equity. Banks are the same story as in the United States and Europe; therefore, it will not have a further explanation because the topic has already been covered. Business angels, as in the United States, are taxed favorably in the United Kingdom. There are some experiences with PPPs in the UK, but not as much as in the US, where there is the SBIC program; in the UK, there are just a few players functioning locally. What is particularly intriguing and novel in the UK system is the concept of VCT (venture capital trust).

A venture capital trust is a vehicle that was established not long ago with the passage of a particular law in 1997. It began as a UK phenomenon, but today there is proof that the venture capital trust has evolved into a type of format. VCTs are becoming increasingly popular in India, one of the world's largest markets, but in this case, the focus will be made only on the UK market.

A venture capital trust is an unusual and distinctive vehicle whose goal is to unite retail investors with outstanding private equity. This is novel because when closed-end funds have been discussed, it has been underlined that private equity investors are often extremely large. The goal of a venture capital trust is to entice a retail investor to the private equity market. To comprehend this vehicle, it is essential to grasp an ancient institution in the UK market: the concept of trust.

A trust is a vehicle into which a person known as the settlor can place assets. The management of these assets is delegated to someone else, who is designated as the trustee, and the trust is required to generate profit and benefits in favor of a beneficiary. Trusts were established in the Middle Ages and were used for a variety of purposes in the United Kingdom and around the world. Entrepreneurs, for example, frequently used it to protect themselves during wartime or to arrange succession within a family firm correctly. The concept of trust is employed for private equity in a venture capital trust.

The concept is that the settlor is not "someone" but rather a retail person. Retailers and investors are simply depositing cash into trusts rather than assets. The trustee is not "someone else" but a management firm. The management company will manage this money to invest in venture capital and private equity, where the beneficiaries are retail investors. What's fascinating is that every time a retail investor invests, he or she receives a certificate, which is then published on the London Stock Exchange. This ensures a high degree of liquidity for retail investors interested in investing in private equity. Some of the last features are related to the fact that venture capital trusts must spend at least 70% of their cash on private equity and venture capital. Another part is related to the fact that retail individuals are willing to gain many tax benefits in doing so.

It is a one-of-a-kind mix, and it is probably the greatest and most effective in the world, combining retail investing with private business, as is typical of private equity.

By Killian Helf

General Tax Overview

Everything necessary to know about legal entities participating in private equity has been covered in this chapter two. Still, to comprehensively cover all the central themes for a total understanding of private equity investors, this chapter must be concluded by covering the complex topic of taxation. Taxation is complicated because it varies by country. Unfortunately, when it comes to laws, it is too broad to cover all of them in this book. So, an outline of the main factor would be highlighted to comprehend taxation on a general basis. To understand tax, a look at two different perspectives is essential.

On the one hand, identifying which part is involved in the taxation of the private equity market is essential. There are three different players: the investor, the vehicle that invests in private equity, and the company receiving money, also called the venture backed.

On the other hand, these three players are impacted differently as they all have different roles. There is five possible "area" where the taxation takes place.

The first "area" which can be impacted by taxation is the capital gains taxation. Only two of the three players are concerned about these taxes. It is relevant for the legal entity investing in private equity and the investors putting their money into the legal entity. When it comes to capital gains taxation for entities engaging in private equity, there is evidence of three separate methods worldwide.

The first method is the flat tax mechanism, which states that a vehicle must pay less tax than other countries' legal organizations. It is what happened, for example, to closed-end funds in Europe, where most countries' closing funds pay a tax rate of 20%, which is often lower than the corporate tax they have in that country.

The second technique is known as tax transparency. It is a specific circumstance in which the flat tax is 0%. The vehicle does not pay taxes, and all costs and income are passed on to the investor. Venture capital funds demonstrate tax transparency in the United States and the United Kingdom, as well as an SBIC in the United States.

The final instance is known as PEX (participation exemption). It is a method that reduces taxation on certain types of investments in equity that the vehicle makes. What happened in Italy, the Netherlands, Ireland, and Luxembourg for investment firms investing in private equity is a good illustration of the participation exemption.

However, capital gains taxes are also significant for investors that invest in a closed-end fund, an SBIC, a venture capital trust, or a venture capital fund. It is impossible to provide obvious criteria in this scenario. Still, it can be stated that in most countries, there is a distinction between whether the investor is a corporation, a legal body, or a private individual and another contrast between whether the investor is domestic or foreign.

The second "area" concerns the case of dividend taxation; it is less relevant because private equity business is not to receive dividends but to receive capital gains. In this case, fortunately, the mechanisms for legal entities and investors are the same as those mentioned for capital gains taxation.

The third "area" that taxation impacts are the Incentive programs for entrepreneurs and R&D. These are applicable solely for the company requiring financing from venture-backed companies in which PEIs will invest in this situation. The concept is straightforward. If a startup is launching in a country where incentives for R&D and entrepreneurs are more important, there will almost certainly be much more investment in venture capital. For incentives to startups and R&D, there is evidence of three different mechanisms around the world.

The first mechanism is the concept of markdown, where the assumption is that if the firm runs a startup or invests in R&D, the corporation benefits from a discount. This means that the tax rate will be reduced.

The second approach addresses shadow cost. A corporation obtains a premium if it establishes a startup or invests in R&D. In most cases, shadow costs imply that the company receives more significant expenses, reducing taxation within the PNL.

Finally, a tax credit is the third mechanism possible. A tax credit is a voucher, with the company getting a portion of the fixed assets required to establish the startup or a piece of the R&D expense. Tax credits serve as a voucher that a corporation can utilize to reduce its tax burden not just in one year but yearly.

The final "area" impacted by taxation is connected to the debt-to-equity ratio incentive or tax. This technique is only applicable for the company seeking finance, which has implications for the venture-backed enterprise. In this case, there are only mechanisms across the world.

The first is called thin capitalization. Thin capitalization limits the company's capacity to employ loan interest rates to reduce taxation. In some ways, it is an indirect incentive to collect equity. In Germany or Italy, for example, there are thin caps.

The other, far more potent, is DIT, or dual income taxation. DIT's goal is to provide tax breaks if the company raises funds through shares. And in this instance, having DIT is a powerful incentive for the corporation to use private equity.

So, to sum up, when taxation is mentioned, there are three distinct players and five distinct areas of impact that must be kept in mind.

New Viable Solutions

Private equity, like the other sector in finance, never misses an opportunity to adapt and tweak its process to fit with the latest trends, and so to do that, innovation is required. Innovation will bring new solutions, and so in a sense, the creation of new entities eager to participate in private equity. Now that an overview of the European Union, the United States, and the United Kingdom markets have been covered. Four attractive possible solutions or trends that may be useful in the future will be developed.

The first new solution is the private debt fund. The concept of a private debt fund is quite basic. It uses vehicles like those covered previously (Closed-end funds, venture capital funds, and investment firms). Investing in private debt rather than private equity is a new trend worldwide. Private debt funds are mainly connected to the fact that in Europe, there is a significant tendency where corporations need to collect more and more money for debt by utilizing the market rather than the banking system. This means that firms will have to issue a lot more bonds. For companies listed on the stock exchange, it is relatively easy to do, they press the button, and the bonds are listed on the stock exchange. However, most enterprises are SMEs, so these companies cannot access the stock exchange. They must sell their bonds to individual investors. Some private equity investors have understood the business and developed the knowledge to know exactly what they need to do when a company is not listed on the public exchange. This type of private equity investor creates an ideal match in specific ways. Many managers, particularly in Europe, are establishing private equity funds dedicated to acquiring private debt.

Crowdfunding is the second solution and the second trend. It is a very digital, modern, and interesting concept. Crowdfunding is a web-based platform that allows various parties, such as private individuals, businesses, and institutions, to initiate a call for funds with a wide range of options. Young individuals willing to incur fees for a trip and launch a fundraising campaign through their friends or a hospital ready to purchase a particular machine to launch a program can also be considered.

Also, venture capital and private equity can be used through crowdfunding, in which companies, particularly those in the first or second stages of their life cycle, post a call on the internet to raise funds. (I am not sure that this technic is effective, but I have not found any paper to support or not my point of view. However, I am convinced that it works effectively for charitable or other purposes). Crowdfunding is mainly used for people who already have a community and are willing to launch a business. Nevertheless, this solution grows a bit more each year thanks to the number of platforms providing this service for retailer investors. However, from a professional investor's point of view, the efficiency of this method still needs to be proved. It cannot be yet considered a reliable and sustainable way to raise money.

The third solution concerns venture philanthropy. Venture philanthropy, like private debt, is a scenario in which well-known private equity vehicles, such as venture capital funds, closed-end funds, and so on, decide to invest primarily in firms with a significant social impact. For example, they may invest in firms that provide social housing or enterprises that offer health care to the underprivileged. These examples can be considered as companies having a significant societal influence. Venture philanthropy seeks to fund these types of businesses using the exact mechanisms as private equity. Still, investors and managers are willing to accept a lower profit level in management fees, carried interest, and capital gains for investors in exchange for the ability to sustain a socially beneficial activity.

The final solution is SPAC (a special purpose acquisition company). This trend began in the United States about 15 years ago and was highly successful. It only arrived more or less five years ago in Europe. A SPAC is an empty shell; simply, it is an SPV. In this SPV, there are promoters of an idea, and these promoters must have 20% of the company's equity. They list the company on the stock exchange to collect the other 80% from the market. It is strange because a new company is listed on the stock exchange with people willing to invest, and on the asset side, there is only cash. However, the SPAC can collect money only to make one investment, for example, a private equity investment to buy another company. If the SPAC succeeds in doing that, the outcome is that the SPAC is going to merge with the target company. If the SPAC does not achieve that, investors who have decided to invest through the IPO in the SPAC will receive their money back. As practitioners say, SPAC is a one-shot vehicle, investing only one time in private equity, but the impact could be significant because they raise money through the stock exchange.

By Killian Helf

Concrete Application

Now that all the general notions of taxation and liabilities structures have been covered, a real case of the carried interest management fee mechanism application would help to have a concrete understanding of how it works, such as the mechanism of profit-sharing between managers and investors. The example would be based on a closed-end fund managed by an AMC.

Firstly, some inputs are required. The most important one is the one related to the amount of the management fee. In this case, the management fee is 2%. The hurdle rate is 8%, and the current interest rate is 30%. The closed-end fund's pledged capital is 400 million euros. Last but not least, the percentage of managers is 2% (this 2% is based on the fact that the AMC is based in Europe and so it is required by law. In the case that the fund would be in US/UK, it would be 1%).

To apply the carried interest formula and calculate the return for both managers and investors. Other figures related to the development of investment for the closed-end fund will be necessary. The table (figure 1) shows 11 years' worth of results. Eleven years is used although the maturity of a closed-end fund is ten years, it is up to the managers to decide if it makes sense to run the investment for an additional three years. The presumption in this scenario is that managers choose to use one more year to wind up the fund's activities.

| | | Investment period | | | | | | Divestment period | | | | Extra | |
| | | Draw-downs | | | | | | | | | | | |
	Years	1	2	3	4	5	6	7	8	9	10	11	Total
(+)	Draw-downs	100	200	100									400
(-)	Investments	80	190	130	180	310	360	100	200	50	0		1600
(+)	Divestments	0	0	40	200	320	370	100	250	500	600	700	3080
(-)	Management fee	8	8	8	8	8	8	8	8	8	8	8	88
	Cash	12	14	16	28	30	32	24	66	508	1100	1792	

Figure 1: Fund overview across years

The first line is name drawdowns; drawdowns are a legal necessity in the first three years. In this case, 100 million euros are raised in the first year, 200 million euros in the second year, and another 100 million euros in the third year.

The investments are found on the second line. The closed-end fund instantly begins investing money in year one and continues its activity until year nine. There are many investments in years ten and eleven since management must focus on quitting the investment in those years.

The third line symbolizes divestment. Divestment entails managing the exit of all transactions. In this situation, there are no exits in the first two years, so there are no divestments. However, there are divestments from year number three to year number eleven.

Line four reflects the management charge, set at 2%. The closed-end fund has a capitalization of 400 million Euros, which means that managers receive 8 million Euros from the fund each year.

The fifth and last line represents the quantity of money. This is significant because the total quantity of cash equals the final amount of the closed-end fund in year 11. That is, the fund started with 400 million Euros in this closed-end fund, and in year 11, managers opted to close the closed-end fund, leaving them with 1,792 million Euros in cash.

The challenge now is how to divide this large sum of money between the managers and the investors. To accomplish so, the notion of carried interest must be employed. Although the formula is always the same, it can be used in two different ways. The first method is known as the global IRR strategy.

Case 1: Global IRR			
Data of the fund		**Return for Managers & Investors**	
Fund global IRR	348%		
Net global IRR	340%	Gross return for managers (GPs)	5100%
Carried interest	102%	Gross return for investors (LPs)	346%
For managers (GPs)	**408**	Yearly return for managers (GPs)	**48,17%**
For investors (LPs)	**1384**	Yearly return for investors (LPs)	**14,73%**

Figure 2: Global IRR method

Case 1 is the worldwide IRR strategy. To begin the global IRR approach, the fund's global IRR must be computed. The formula which needs to be used is the global one. That means the difference between the total amount of money, 1,792 million euros, less the committed capital, 400 million euros, divided by the committed capital, 400 million euros. This means that the fund's return is 348 percent.

Taking the hurdle rate out, the net worldwide IRR is 340 percent. When the carried interest, which is 30%, is multiplied, the result is 102 percent carried interest. This percentage must now be transformed. 102 percent of a sum of money when the sum of money is for the management. The norm is to calculate the return on a global basis of 400 million euros.

And if 400 million euros is doubled by 102%. The total amount is 408 million euros, which is the amount of money allocated to the management.

The amount of money for the investors is between 1,792 million and 408 million Euros. The annual return for the managers who invested 2% of the 400 million Euros and the investors who invested 400 million euros can also be computed.

The second method is known as the yearly IRR strategy.

Case 2: Yearly IRR			
Data of the fund		**Return for Managers & Investors**	
Fund yearly IRR	16,2%		
Net yearly IRR	8,2%	Gross return for managers (GPs)	1527,9%
Carried interest	2,45%	Gross return for investors (LPs)	414,44%
For managers (GPs)	**122,23**	Yearly return for managers (GPs)	**31,34%**
For investors (LPs)	**1669,76**	Yearly return for investors (LPs)	**17,13%**

Figure 3: Yearly IRR method

However, the yearly IRR technique can calculate the carried interest in the second situation. The opening of the story is the same in both cases. The global IRR of the funds must be calculated, but the global technique is not used, and it is only computed by using the IRR concept.

As can be seen, the return in this situation is 16.2 percent. When the net yearly IRR is calculated, the result is 8.2%. Then by multiplying 8.2% by 30%, the amount of return for the managers is found, which in this case is 2.45%.

Once the return for managers is found (2.45% in this case), the amount of money using the IRR once more must be computed. The amount of money will be lower than in the first example, and it will be roughly 122 million euros.

The amount of money available to investors will be the difference between 1,792 and 122 million Euros. As it occurs, in the first scenario, it is possible to compute the yearly return for both the managers and the investors.

In both cases, formulas are used without catching up. The carried interest is determined by subtracting the final IRR from the hurdle rate. It is also feasible to calculate the identical findings with catch-up. In this instance, the carried interest is calculated on the amount of the fund's IRR rather than the difference. The requirement for doing so is that the fund's return exceeds the hurdle rate.

Chart for IRR	1	2	3	4	5	6	7	8	9	10	11
IRR	-400	0	0	0	0	0	0	0	0	0	1792
Case 1 Investment GPs	-8	0	0	0	0	0	0	0	0	0	408
Investment LPs	-100	-200	-100	0	0	0	0	0	0	0	1384
Case 2 Investment GPs	-8	0	0	0	0	0	0	0	0	0	122.23
Investment LPs	-100	-200	-100	0	0	0	0	0	0	0	1669.76

Figure 4: Overview of the two IRR case

Chapter 3:

An Overview Of The Managerial Process

By Killian Helf

The Managerial Process

It is time to look inside the mind of a private equity investor. There is evidence of a wide range of legal entities throughout the world. For example, in Europe, there are closed-end funds or investment firms, whereas in the United States, there are venture capital funds and SBICs, and in the United Kingdom, there are venture capital trusts. However, the legal entities are incredibly diverse as it is based on two separate players. The operations of the run-in private equity firm behind the legal entities are identical. For every private equity firm, managers manage other players' money by investing it in certain legal companies. As a result, the management of a private equity business is the same in any legal organization wherever in the world. Thanks to having a look at the managerial process make sense.

The managerial process is the day-to-day work of managers who handle investors' money. To highlight the managerial process's characteristics, criteria that academia and practitioners enjoy using to qualify the daily life of legal entities investing in private equity must be employed.

Fundraising, investing, managing & monitoring, and exiting are the four activities that qualify the managerial process. There are four activities to choose from. Even though the first action, fundraising, is entirely independent of the other three. As mentioned previously, fundraising is a precursor to establishing a legal corporation. For example, in a closed-end fund, an asset management business has one and a half years to persuade investors to invest in the closed-end fund. The same is true for venture capital funds in the United States, where general partners have one year to convince limited partners to invest their money. Fundraising is distinct from the other three activities.

However, if the managers can obtain the total amount of money, they can reach time 0. The legal entity can begin the activity at this point, and the other three activities can occur. Every day, managers face the problem of investing the money of investors, which is the investing phase. Every day managers face the challenge of managing and monitoring their investments in specific companies, as well as the extremely complex subject of exiting. Remember that exiting is the only method for a private equity firm to achieve a capital gain or an IRR. If these four operations shall be summed up, the fundraising would be the most challenging phase because general partners and management must persuade investors to put money into the vehicle. This procedure might be completely unregulated, as it is in the United States and the United Kingdom, or it could be supervised, as it is in the European Union, when running, for example, a closed-end fund.

As stated, the first step is fundraising, if the managers or general partners can persuade investors, the fund would finally be able to launch its activity, and the time 0 would be reached.

Then once the money is raised, the management has to decide which company they will invest in. This step represents the second one called "investing." To know if a company is financially speaking interesting, they must examine the organization and determine whether the company's value or business model makes sense. Then if managers or general partners opt to invest, they must discuss the essential qualities. Once all these points have been covered, the management takes a decision; if this one is to invest, the third step of managing & monitoring would be necessary.

The third phase is management & monitoring. Managing & monitoring means that the private equity investor has become a shareholder of the venture-backed company due to the decision to invest. Being a shareholder is difficult since the investor must remain on the board of directors, where he/she must communicate with the entrepreneur and support and sustain the company's daily operations. However, if management and monitoring are successful, the final phase begins.

The final phase is the exiting phase, which entails selecting another investor who wishes to purchase company shares in which the private equity investors have opted to invest. This is not easy because the company is not on the stock exchange. So, there is a pricing and liquidity problem. Still, it is a fundamental activity because the private equity firm can only make a capital gain through the exit via capital gains.

Fundraising

The first activity that qualifies the managerial process is fundraising. It is difficult for any manager in any country throughout the world. Because, in the fundraising process, managers or general partners must persuade investors to commit their money for an extended period of time. In a closed-end or venture capital fund in the United States or the United Kingdom, when investors decide to commit their money for ten years, they cannot do anything since the managers manage the money, and they cannot leave the investment. As a result, it is a highly important and critical decision for the investor.

Fundraising is a well-organized activity centered mostly on four different components.

The first component is the creation or launching of the business idea. This step implies persuading investors to put their money into a private equity firm. The development of a business idea begins with something casual, known as testing the waters. Testing the waters is determining, in a very secret and informal manner, if investors want to commit their money to a specific private equity vehicle. Imagine that an investor seeks to form a closed-end fund focusing on startups. Before he/she starts the activity, he/she needs to know if the community of investors is exciting or not by this idea; by pooling his/her network and, more generally, investors, he/she will be able to get a general opinion of the current trend regarding this type of investment. If their opinion toward investing in a company is positive, the investor continues; otherwise, the investor must adjust his/her business plan and put it in another cluster. If the testing of the waters is positive, establishing the business idea could become a little more formal. In addition, managers or general partners are usually required to create an information memorandum. An info memorandum is a document that consists of a series of slides in which management describes all the features of the vehicle they intend to launch. That implies, for example, they must declare the size of the fund. What is the carried interest mechanism? How much is the management fee? What are the portfolio management criteria? So, many factors qualify the private equity investor's business offer. Assuming, once again, that the investor's emotion is good. If the fund that the investor wants to launch is in Europe, he/she must go to the supervisor and request permission to begin the activity. The information memorandum is immediately transformed into an internal code of activity.

In contrast, if the creator of the fund wants to launch it in US/UK because venture capital funds do not require clearance, in this case, the information memorandum is simply changed into an LPA (limited partnership agreement). Even if the content is identical, the profile is different because an internal code of activity is a document approved by a supervisor. At the same time, an LPA is a formal document, but any supervisor reviewed it.

If managers can get to this point, they have a formal document or contract in their hands and can begin the second activity called "selling job."

The purpose and goal of a selling job are to convince investors to sign a contract, which is a letter of commitment, rather than to give an opinion or grasp their attitude. The commitment letter states how much money a specific investor wants to commit to the closed-end or venture capital fund. Selling a job is usually something very confidential and private. In most cases, because investors are high net worth individuals, insurance companies or investment banks are based on one-on-one meetings. But in some cases, the selling job could be organized into meetings, not precisely in road shows, as happens for IPOs, but in discussions with many investors involved. In the United

Kingdom or the United States, where venture capital funds can leverage, there is a third activity: debt raising.

The third component is "debt raising" in this context, it attempts to persuade the banking system to lend money, not as limited partners, but merely as a financier. It is difficult because, on the one hand, the investor has to persuade investors to lend money to his/her vehicle, and to provide money, they want to know if the banking system is willing to lend debt. On the other hand, he/she must persuade the financial system to lend money through debt and want to know if the limited partners are on board.

The greater the general partner's reputation, the easier the job. On the contrary, if the general partners are unknown and their track record is not incredible, it can be challenging to convince both the banking system and limited partners to commit their money. However, if fundraising is successful in one year in the United States and the United Kingdom, the period where the phase is closing will be reached.

Finally, the fourth and final component, "closing," occurs. It signifies that the private equity firm has collected the complete sum. That is significant since the closing activity marks the conclusion of the fundraising, and that exact moment indicates time 0. The PEI can begin investing its funds at time zero. In many circumstances, the closing may not be fortunate, which means that the PE firm did not receive the whole amount of money. Closing has a different meaning in this scenario. Closing implies that operations must be ceased and that the fund can no longer launch PE investments.

The Decision-Making Phase

If fundraising is successful, the managerial process's second activity can start, represented by investing. It is a clear and straightforward term since it implies investing money of investors across different structures for a given period (approximatively ten years as seen for closed-end and venture capital funds). However, investing becomes a bit more complex as investment refers to two different activities.

Firstly, investing entails deciding whether or not to invest in a specific company, referred to as decision-making. However, if the decision to invest in a company is taken, a second deal-making process begins. Deal-making is negotiating a contract to invest with a particular company.

Concretely if an investor scouts and identifies a specific company. He/She believes this company is excellent and intends to invest. This is decision-making, but it is another story to design the contract to invest in this company, where building the contract includes calculating the number of shares the investor needs to acquire, establishing rights and corporate governance rules, and so on. The task is complex, and even if the result is favorable, the deal-making process might effectively halt the investment choice.

The focus now is on understanding how the decision-making process works. Some authors and practitioners like to say not only decision-making but also deal flow to convey that the decision-making process aims to generate, hopefully, a massive flow of opportunities in which the PEI can contemplate investing.

The decision-making process is divided into several steps. Every step involves a varied involvement of the various actors operating in the PE vehicle. Remember that in a PE vehicle, there are managers, or general partners, who are the major participants and actors. Still, a technical committee also assists the general partners in doing their job. There is also an advisory firm that advises the general partners on how to conduct their jobs. To summarize, there is various participation of these different players working in a PE firm in the decision-making process.

The first step is "origination," which means originating (creating) investing ideas. Typically, origination is driven by two distinct factors. The first driver is mainly related to the fact that the origination is unplanned. Because by being a PEI, the entire business system knows that the PEI has a lot of money, and a lot of people will come knocking on his/her door every day, offering investment to him/her. The private equity investor must have the ability to sort through a large number of bids. And determine which proposal makes the most sense?

On the other way around, origination is based on proactive activity. Proactive means that general partners must run and walk into the market and potential scout businesses; they are definitely paid to do that. In origination, general partners, however, are supported by the advisory company and the technical committee. At the end of the process of origination, a second activity starts.

The screening activity is the second activity. Screening entails reviewing all the proposals or dossiers received by the PE firm and determining which type of dossier and/or proposal makes the most sense. As mentioned earlier, historical data suggests that screening involves rejecting 90 of the 100 offers received by a private equity firm. It is a polite way of saying 90 proposals are garbage, and only ten make sense to study further.

The general partners are entirely responsible for the screening activity. They are hired to do just that. The screening produces a tiny number of proposals and dossiers that warrant further investigation.

The next activity is due diligence and appraisal. Due diligence and appraisal entail analyzing the company strategy, checking numbers, and determining whether the business idea is viable. It takes a long time, and that is why firstly, a screening action is needed. Only a few people have the resources to conduct an appraisal and due diligence on 100 dossiers. It makes sense to conduct value due diligence on only 10 out of 100. The valuation and due diligence are committed to excluding alternative ideas that are ineffective. The result of appraisal and due diligence is a small number of offers where the rating assignment makes sense.

Rating assignment is the fourth step in the decision-making phase; it consists of assigning a rating to the dossier received by the PEI. Where the rating given is essential for understanding the level of risk, but it may also be helpful if money needs to collect through debt collection. For example, in a leveraged buyout, when the SPV must be financed with debt, knowing the rating ahead of time is fundamental since if the rating is not good, activities must be halted.

Step number five is the general partners leading the negotiation; it is a negotiation with the company to see whether there is enough room to run the investment. A crucial negotiation topic, for example, is the company's value.

The goal of an entrepreneur is to maximize the value of his/her enterprise to raise as much money as possible. Still, at the same time, the goal of the private equity investor is to minimize its value to have a bigger gain when he/she disposes of the firm. This negotiation can become difficult quickly, and many deals will not occur due to it. However, the final phase can be reached if the negotiation is successful.

The final phase is the decision to invest. A global decision must be made between the Board of general partners or the Board of directors in case of an AMC. Investing money does not simply give money to the company but begins the second step of the investment activity, which is deal-making.

The "Deal-Making" Phase

Deal-making represents the other side of the investing process. Suppose the decision-making process was positive, where positive signifies a thumbs up from the AMC's or general partners' boards. Another story begins, this time about deal-making. In a word, deal-making is writing, and hopefully signing, a contract between the PEI and the firm in which they find the correct balance between the company's need for money and the PEI's expectation of IRR and capital gain. Finding this balance is complex, which is why it is called "deal-making.". In a sense, the deal-making activity is founded on three pillars.

The first idea is the one of targeting; it is mostly based on many decisions that must be negotiated with the organization. For example, the first one is about the investment vehicle; in many circumstances, the PEI will invest in the target firm's equity, but in other cases, the PEI may decide to invest in an SPV rather than the company. The usage of an SPV is mandatory if a replacement financing cluster is done if an IPO is run but also if the goal of the private equity investor is to finance a company for an M&A transaction. All these reasons make the choice of an SPV coherent. However, creating an SVP is difficult because doing so entails deciding to use debt, which requires convincing the banking sector to lend money to the vehicle. The two issues and decisions on the table are whether to conduct a direct investment in the firm or a non-direct investment, utilizing an SPV to invest in the company. Once the decision is taken, the process can continue.

Another common point of negotiation is the number of shares. The number of shares is the percentage of stock the PEI wants to receive. The problem is complicated because several things must be avoided.

In many circumstances, having a tiny number of shares, such as 1%, 2%, or 3%, is useless because this amount is not significant enough to stay in the firm. Having more than 50%, on the other hand, indicates that the private equity investor is the most important shareholder. The PEI is the firm's owner, which is not always a good thing because he/she needs an entrepreneur as the company's owner who has the necessary passion for driving the company. These reasons make the discussion about the percentage of shares difficult.

Once the targeting process is done, the second pillar, the liability profile, must be covered. The liabilities profile is the liability side of the company's balance sheet in which the PEI intends to invest. Two different judgments need to be made when the liability profile is mentioned.

The first judgment is associated with the concept of syndication strategy. According to the syndication plan, the PEI will syndicate the business with one or more other PEIs. It may appear weird because the PEI invested significant money in screening the market, investigating a company, and evaluating it. So why would a PEI give a business to another PEI? The explanation could be that there is a lack of money from the PEI, or the deal is so large that the PEI does not have enough money to proceed with the investment, and the logical decision could be to try to syndicate the firm with another PEI.

The second judgment concerns the concept of debt issuing. It entails taking a hands-on approach and assisting the company or SPV in issuing debt, where debt means issuing bonds on the market once it is a very large deal. Or, on the contrary, negotiating loans with the banking system to finance the company or SPV again.

The final phase, "engagement," begins once the liability profile is completed. Engagement entails establishing the rules that govern the presence of private equity in the company's equity. This final pillar is comprised of three distinct activities.

The first, share categories, refer to the rights the PEI obtains by purchasing the company's stock. One option is to issue ordinary shares, which is extremely frequent, but PEI, for example, may want to receive preferred stock. Preferred stocks are distinguished by additional rights relating to the shares, such as a put option under which the PEI can sell the shares to the PE. Another popular type of preferred stock is one that allows for extra voting rights. For example, if a PEI owns 20% of the firm, but these stocks are preferred, this 20% of shares could represent 40% - 49% of voting rights on the board of directors.

The paying policy represents the second aspect. According to the payment rules, the PEI can purchase new shares or must also purchase existing shares of the entrepreneur. Returning to the first chapter, private equity is dependent on funding. That is, private equity solely depends on acquiring new shares. However, if the entrepreneur is particularly powerful or the deal is very crucial, the PEI may be required to purchase shares of the entrepreneur to return money to the entrepreneur.

The final part concerns governance rules. Governance rules imply negotiating the board's operation to ensure and publicize the ability of the private equity investor to interact with and drive the company. For example, the board of directors has the option of having the chairman on the board, and the scheduling of board meetings are all instances of qualifying corporate governance standards.

Managing and Monitoring: Supporting the Company

If the deal-making process is successful, the PEI becomes a company shareholder. That implies another activity, and this activity is known as the managerial process, also called MM. It is a different story because if the decision to invest is made, the PEI becomes one of the company's shareholders. The PEI's goal is now completely different because the PEI has to stay in the company and help the company generate more value. Significantly, the PEI immediately begins looking for a new strategy to exit the company to create a capital gain. Managing and monitoring are difficult because when the PEI decides to invest, he/she faces significant price and liquidity challenges. Managing and monitoring entail providing the ideal conditions for a smooth exit from the company.

The things must be comprehended gradually. Managing and monitoring are two fundamental cornerstones of an activity. On the one hand, private equity must assist the company in generating value, and this assistance might take several forms. It depends, for example, on whether the PEI takes a hands-on or hands-off attitude. The number of shares held determines it too. In any scenario, the PE needs the company to generate greater value. On the other hand, private equity must safeguard the company's worth. It appears simple, yet it is pretty complex.

For example, managing and monitoring imply that the private equity investor and the corporation are married. They both want to produce value; thus, they have the same aim, but their decisions could be very different. There is a significant problem of divergence of opinion in management and monitoring.

Some examples can help to understand this purpose. Assume a private equity firm wishes to invest in a company. The company plan is excellent, and the management is outstanding. Everything works perfectly, but suppose the entrepreneur decides to make a completely different decision and conduct an M&A in a foreign country the following day. It is not in the business plan, but the entrepreneur wants to execute it. A conflict may arise because the PEI wants the company to remain compliant with the business plan, and to make the decision to run an M&A means that it could probably generate more value in the long run. Still, in the short and the medium term, this could affect the value created, and the PEI cannot remain forever in the company and needs to exit. To avoid that, the PEI and the company in which the PEI is invested try to work together.

Firstly, on the operational side to help the organization generate greater value. For example, a PEI can provide service to help the board's structuration to optimize the company's chance of success, create a framework, or develop the corporate governance. But he/she can also bring his/her experience to help the company build its activities from a more operational aspect; these are simple examples from a non-exhaustive list of the PEI's role in a company.

Secondly on the hiring manager. Hiring management means that firms in many circumstances require new, better management. In many cases, a company, particularly a small or medium-sized one or a startup, lacks the potential to recruit management from outside. This is an excellent assignment for the PEI.

Another activity can be the performance review or performance system. In many circumstances, a firm's accountability, auditing, IT, and information systems do not function well, or the company does not have this system. Again, the PEI's duty is to assist the firm in purchasing or establishing the appropriate processes to help the company generate added value.

Another type of assistance is related to relationship management. In many situations, the PEI has an extensive network of banking system knowledge, advisors, suppliers, and consumers. A fundamental job of the PEI is to provide the firm with access to this vast network, thereby multiplying the company's value.

Mentoring is a final but crucial activity. Mentoring implies that the private equity must be available to the entrepreneur 24 hours a day, seven days a week. It signifies everything since, as already stated, the company and the PEI are married. And it is natural from the entrepreneur's perspective to expect that the PEI will be able to support the entrepreneur's decision at any time. On many occasions, judgments are tied not just to commercial difficulties but also highly personal issues. However, the role of a general partner, or the management of an AMC, is always to help the entrepreneur.

This varied range of activities shows that the relationship between a PEI and a company is much more than a contract. It is a relationship in which the PEI qualified its presence not only in terms of money but also in terms of advice. And being an advisor is critical to the success of the PEI himself or herself.

By Killian Helf

Managing and Monitoring: Covenants Usage

Enhancing the firm's value creation is one part of managing and monitoring. Still, the other side of the story is represented by the need to protect the value the company has generated. This is a critical need for the PEI since he/she only has a limited period and must exit while maximizing its financial gain. As a result, safeguarding the value created within the organization is critical. Protecting value is complex, and best practices of PEIs from across the world suggest that the ideal solution may be to negotiate, inserting several covenants into the relationship between the PEI and the enterprise.

Covenants govern the duties and rights of the PEI and the venture-backed enterprise. The list of covenants comprises nine processes that need to be kept in mind to grasp virtually everything about the subject of value protection.

Lockup represents the first covenant. A lockup is a system that prevents one of the shareholders from selling shares before a specific date. It is mainly useful in new firms, for example. One of the concerns for the PEI in a startup business is that the entrepreneur will sell his or her shares immediately. That could be risky because the PEI agreed to invest because of the entrepreneur's skill, and if the entrepreneur decides to leave and sell his or her shares, it will be a disaster for the PEI. The lockup mechanism allows the PEI to stop, decrease, and mitigate this type of danger.

The permitted transfer represents the second mechanism. A permitted transfer is a more complex lockup in that one shareholder can only sell its shares with the approval of the other shareholder. Consider the following scenario: a PEI decides to invest in a firm. The approved transfer allows the entrepreneur to sell a specific number of shares or the total number of shares with the consent of the PEI. It is a method of mitigating the risk of the entrepreneur's exit.

The staging technique represents the third mechanism. The staging strategy is quite common in the United States and is especially popular for new firms. It is based on the idea that a PEI will deliver money in distinct tranches. And each tranche is only delivered if the company can meet specified metrics at particular milestones. Consider another startup. Startups are extremely risky endeavors. One tale may be that the PEI will pay the entire sum at time zero. Assume an investor has 50 million euros. With the staging technique, the idea is to say, the PEI is going to give the entrepreneur 50 million euros, but the 50 million euros will be split into five tranches of 10 million euros. The only condition for receiving the next tranche of 10 million euros is that the company meets specific numbers in the business plan. The staging technique is a collection of instruments designed to decrease risk and produce the correct incentive for the organization to achieve specified outcomes.

Stock options represent mechanism number four. Stock options are particularly prevalent in the investment banking sector, as well as in private equity. What exactly are stock options? A stock option is a covenant that allows a shareholder to purchase new shares at a discounted price. It is useful again, for example, in a startup in its early stages or in any situation where the entrepreneur is extremely important. The PEI incentivizes the entrepreneur to work hard in the company through a stock option system. Because the entrepreneur will labor a lot, he/she can acquire shares at a very low price while the share's value increases. This strategy is prevalent in situations where the PEI holds the majority of shares and the entrepreneur has the minority. And there is a chance that the entrepreneur will not be motivated to work in the company.

Callable and puttable securities represent the fifth mechanism.

Callable and puttable securities are shares that have embedded call and/or put options. Puttable security is the most famous example. Puttable security is one in which private equity buys shares with a put option. That means the private equity firm can sell the shares to the entrepreneur. Shares may also be callable. Callable could imply that the entrepreneur has a call option. That means he/she can purchase the shares from the PEI and thereby sacking the PEI. Callable and puttable securities are often used in private equity firms to identify several exit strategies from the marriage of the entrepreneur, the company, and the PE.

The tag-along right represents Covenant number six. Tag-along right is a guarantee for minority PEIs. It gives the private equity investor the right to sell the shares to the entrepreneur at the same price the entrepreneur will sell them. It is an extremely attractive exit strategy because if the entrepreneur sells shares to someone else, the PEI can sell the shares at the same price.

The drag-along right symbolizes the seventh covenant. With the drag-along right, the PEI can ask the entrepreneur to sell its shares at the same price as the PEI. What is the significance of the drag-along? It is significant because, with drag-along, the PEI can sell 100 percent of the company's shares while still holding 100 percent. And, if the PEI can sell all of his/her shares, he/she can negotiate a fantastic price.

Covenant Number Eight express the right of first refusal. It means that the PEI has the right to buy the shares from the entrepreneur at the same price that the entrepreneur will sell to someone else. Essentially, it is a mechanism that the PEI wishes to have in place to protect the value of the number of shares in its portfolio.

The exit ratchet represents the final mechanism. The exit ratchet is a covenant that states that when one shareholder sells shares to another, a percentage of the capital gain be returned to the other shareholder.

That is, for example, the case in which the PEI intends to sell shares. The entrepreneur is extremely powerful, and he/she desires a percentage of the PE's capital gain. Alternatively, if the business is highly successful and the PEI invested heavily in the entrepreneur, and the entrepreneur plans to exit alongside the PEI, the PEI wishes to recoup a portion of the entrepreneur's capital gain as a reward for the significant support that the PEI provided to the company.

Exiting

The final stage of the managerial process is the exit. It is important because departing the PEI can result in a monetary gain or loss. A capital gain equals an IRR and a profit. Returning to chapter one, it has been stated that exiting is extremely tough. It is difficult because private equity investors are different from public equity investors. The stock exchange is available to public equity investors. PEI's face significant pricing and liquidity challenges. It is critical to understand the exit choices available to the PEIs. There are not many options on the table because there are five possibilities while one is pretty poor.

The first one is called the trade sale. The meaning of trade sale is simple: selling the shares to another entrepreneur or company. The principle is simple, yet it is tough to implement in practice. Many businesses do not want their PEI to be sold to another entrepreneur. The first entrepreneur does not wish to share his or her interaction with another.

In many cases of PE investment, the entrepreneur wants the PEI to sign a contract prohibiting trade sales. Looking at market best practices, trade sales are pretty standard in two circumstances. The first is a leveraged buyout. The PEI has the option to sell all of the shares. The second situation is when the PEI has drag-along rights. When the PEI has drag-along rights, it has the option of selling all the shares.

This practice can also be found in PIPE, where the PEI intends to invest in a publicly-traded firm. Because the company is listed on the stock exchange, it is significantly easier to make a trade sale in this scenario.

The buyback represents the second option. Buyback is both simple and popular. The entrepreneur will purchase the shares from the PEI during the repurchase. As a result, one of the most common covenants is represented by puttable shares. The only concern regarding this practice is basic and straightforward, but must be emphasized, is that to conduct a repurchase, the entrepreneur must have adequate money. Signing a covenant with a put option is one of the risks for the PEI. The entrepreneur is delighted to sign a contract, but when the PEI intends to exercise the put option, the entrepreneur lacks sufficient money. If the entrepreneur cannot afford to buy back, discussion begins to cut the price or add other people to the deal to be able to afford it.

The third option is the IPO or the sale following the IPO. Every PEI fantasizes about an IPO because it allows the PEI to maximize its capital gain. But it is important to be pragmatic because statistics show that for every 100 PE deals, only one exit occurs through an IPO. So, an IPO is excellent since it maximizes capital gain, but it is challenging because organizing an IPO requires the proper alignment of stars because the stock exchange must fly. The company must be prepared to go public. The company's business must be glamorous enough to be accepted by the stock exchange, and the entrepreneur must be the ideal person to work with stock exchange investors. It is a challenging combo.

When there is a bubble, it becomes more common in some ways. Going back to 2000 or 2005, when the stock market was soaring, there were many IPOs because of a bubble. If the idea of the bubble is kept away, running an IPO is a difficult, even if exciting, job.

The sale to another PEI represents option number four. In this instance, the PEI will sell to another PEI. The concept is based on the life cycle concept that has previously been explained. Assume a venture capitalist invests in a startup, the firm grows, and the venture capitalist exits by selling its shares to a PEI looking to fund the company during its expansion phase. So, in essence, this notion is founded on the life cycle concept. It is very common, for example, in very efficient and well-organized PE markets, such as the United States, even if it is not so easy to sell to another PEI because the two PEIs have different ideas, the first wants to maximize the value of the exit, that is, the capital gain. In contrast, the other wants to buy it at a very low price because it, too, wants to maximize the future capital gain. Negotiating between two PEI is a difficult task, and it is a difficult story.

Finally, option number five is not an option. It is not something PEI fantasizes about, like an IPO, but it is possible. It is a write-off. A write-off is the cancellation of the stake's value. It occurs when a corporation defaults. For example, with seed and startup financing, there could be a default because the company's financing is risky, or the business strategy is very aggressive. The risk of a flaw is something tangible. There is no way out in this instance. The PEI must deduct the value of the stake. To cancel the value of the share does not necessarily imply a loss of 100 percent of the IRR because the PEI may try to sell some assets, such as the company's brand if it has one.

In this method, the PEI attempts to reduce the number of losses.

Chapter 4:

How To Value A Company

Fundamental of Company Valuation

The final chapter of this book is about company valuation and deal-making. The core of any PE transaction is the valuation of the company. The definition of company valuation is simple because it implies calculating the worth of a firm's equity. It is a very relevant term in PE agreements. It is critical to converting the amount of money that PEI delivers to the company into a specific amount of equity. It is a tricky matter because the amount of equity affects the ability of the PEI to interact with the venture-backed company's corporate governance.

The challenge is figuring out how to compute the equity value. To do that, the corporate finance world already has a theory, so there is no need to develop a new one. The equity value calculation is driven by very solid best practices among practitioners and academics. As a result, a new theory, as mentioned, is not required.

The essential factor is to understand how the idea of equity value is implemented in private equity transactions. It is important to catch that the issue of equity value in private equity acquisitions is tied to two distinct moments.

The first occasion occurs at time zero when the PEI decides to invest. And at time 0, there is a problem with estimating the equity value since it is needed to determine how much equity the private equity investor will acquire.

However, there is a second point at which estimating the equity value is critical, which is at the time of exit.

So, the same notion developed on two different occasions. Even if these two occasions do not show a correlation at the first glance there are indeed linked since the difference between the equity value at time

0 and the time of exit, as well as the duration in which private equity decides to stay in the firm, affect the IRR of the entire investment. This principle is so significant that the PEI's activity in many negotiations is to negotiate the price of the entrance extremely hard. In other words, it means minimizing the value of the company's equity.

On the other hand, the PEI's job is to negotiate, in a very tough way, what the amount of equity value at exit is, in this case, not to minimize but to maximize. Now that this overview about the role of evaluating a company has been made, it is essential to recall the fundamentals, the foundations of the notion of equity value, or a firm valuation inside corporate finance.

The most common method of calculating a business's equity value is discounted cash flow, or DCF, where the premise of CF entails calculating the firm's worth simply as the present value of the future cash flows the company is about to generate. To predict future cash flow, a sound business plan is required to apply the calculations; if an investor wants to employ the DCF methodology, he/she must use a well-known formula.

The formula is based on the following concept. The equity value of a company is equal to the sum from T1 to n of the cash flows generated by the company and from time 1 to time n, divided by one plus WACC to power t plus the terminal value at time n minus the net financial position minus the minorities plus the surplus assets.

$$\boxed{\sum_{t=1}^{n} \frac{CF_t}{(1 + WACC^t)} + TV_n} + (SA - M - NFP)$$

Enterprise value is framed in red

From T1 to time usually refer to the availability of the business plan;

the standard practice is to use three, four, or a maximum of five years. When the terminal value at time n is stated, it means at time three, four, or five (depending on data availability). The important thing to understand in this method is that the total of the present value of cash flows plus the terminal value at time n is known as enterprise value. It is relevant since the enterprise value is unaffected by the company's profile qualities or responsibility.

The DCF is frequently used in conjunction with different multiples, which provide a relatively basic idea for private equity investors, regardless of the type of bank or financial institution involved in corporate finance, to compare the evaluation of the equity value produced by DCF to the average equity value of similar deals.

The most common multiples are enterprise value divided by EBITDA, enterprise value divided by EBIT, and enterprise value divided by sales. But two other multiple can be computed to this list. These two are equity value divided by earnings and equity value divided by book value.

The concept of multiples is very similar to buying a flat. When a flat must be bought, the person willing to buy it wants to know the worth of the apartment he/she is going to buy, but he/she also wants to compare this value to previous transactions in the same region in which the investor wants to invest. The same holds for equity value. When an investor wants to buy a company, he/she wants to determine its value using DCF, but he/she also wants to compare it to previous transactions in the market.

Company Valuation: The Pillars of DCF

Something considerably more complicated needs to be now performed; all aspects of the DCF approach must be inspected. That means identifying all the elements that quantify the formula that need to be used to compute equity value.

The first step is based on the total cash flows, where the company's business plan determines cash flows. That means if three, four, or five years are selected, the cash flow must be computed for three, four, or five years.

Cash flow is the difference between EBIT minus income taxes, plus depreciation, minus increasing net working capital, and minus capital expenditure, also known as Capex. This is how cash flow is computed year after year.

Cash flow formula:

$$CF = EBIT - Income.Taxes + Depreciation - Increase.in.net.working.capital - Capex$$

Following cash flow, the concept of WACC must be considered. WACC stands for the weighted average cost of capital, and it is used to assess the cost of the company's liabilities. WACC is the net cost of debt multiplied by debt, divided by debt plus equity, plus the cost of equity multiplied by equity divided by equity plus debt. The concept behind this formula is to determine the cost of the debt, the cost of the equity, and the weighted average.

WACC formula:

$$i_{WACC} = i_d x \frac{D}{D + E} + i_e x \frac{E}{D + E}$$

iwacc= Weighted average cost of capital
id= net cost of debt
D=debt

E=equity
ie=cost of equity

The issue now is to calculate both the cost of debt and the cost of equity, which is a little more complicated.

The net cost of debt is relatively simple because it equals the cost of debt multiplied by one minus t, where t is the corporate tax. Why is it needed to multiply the debt cost by the difference between one and the tax ratio rate? This is related to the fact that corporations have an edge in debt collection in all countries since they pay lower tax rates. This is known as a tax shield.

To determine the cost of debt, statistics are generally used from the company's balance sheet and divide the amount of interest expenses by the quantity of debt.

However, it is also possible to be a bit more sophisticated by determining the cost of each liability per liability. But this method is mainly used in certain balance sheets; there are not many liabilities. Nevertheless, the most common approach to computing the net cost of debt stayed the first one mentioned.

Net cost of debt formula:

$$i_d^* = i_d(1 - t)$$

id= cost of debt
t= corporate taxes

Because equity does not pay interest expenses, the concept of cost of equity is far more sophisticated than the concept of cost of debt.

The cost of equity cannot be calculated using the balance sheet for the cost of debt. As a result, a theory is needed, which is known as the CAPM model. The notion is that the cost of equity is equal to the risk-free rate plus Beta, multiplied by the risk premium, and then subtracted from the risk-free rate. But all these items need to be explained to be useful.

The risk-free interest rate is the interest rate that an investor can earn by investing money in an asset without any risk. It is difficult to find a risk-free investment these days. For instance, the interest rate paid by triple-A bonds is the best practice worldwide. For example, when investing in Germany, the objective is to use the Bund's interest rate as a risk-free rate. Alternatively, if investing in the United States, the concept is to take the interest rate investors earn while investing in US Treasury Bonds. Even if any investment can be considered without risk, the hypostasis of risk-free is based on the government bond. To be simple, it assumed that governments are too big to fail. Even if this idea can be more or less accurate, this stays the best practice to find a risk-free investment.

The risk premium is the average return on investment in a certain stock exchange. For instance, if the cost of equity on a US company wants to be determined, the risk premium based on the average return from investment on the US stock exchange must be computed.

The correlation between a certain stock's price and the entire stock exchange trend is known as Beta. If the correlation is more than one, it suggests that the stock's volatility in which the investor wants to invest is greater than the volatility of the stock exchange itself. But if the Beta is less than one, it signifies that the stock volatility that the investor is targeted is lower than the volatility of the stock exchange itself.

Calculating Beta is easy when it is based on companies listed on the stock exchange, but the private equity company is not listed on the stock exchange. In this instance, calculating the Beta is impossible, and the ideal practice is to use the betas of other companies listed on the stock exchange. This notion is based on the standard that company in the same industry as the venture-backed have relatively similar Beta except for a few unusual circumstances; that is why the Beta of a listed company are used to determine the Beta of the private equity company However, the issue is that, in many circumstances, comparable organizations have liability structures that are fundamentally different from private equity company's liability structure, and this influence may affect the risk of the evaluation itself. As a result, a process known as unlever and relever of the Beta must be carried out.

Unlever the Beta involves removing the comparable company's betas from their liability structure. To find the beta unlever, the betas of similar companies must be divided by one plus one minus T, where T is the tax rate multiplied by debt and divided by equity. After calculating the beta unlever, the result must relate to the private equity company's debt-to-equity ratio.

To do so, calculations to relever Beta are needed. The first step is to multiply beta unlever by one plus one minus T, where T is the taxation rate, multiplied by debt, divided by equity, where the debt-to-equity ratio is one of the private equity companies. This is the whole procedure for calculating the cost of equity.

Unlever of the Beta:

$$\beta_u = \beta / [1 + (1 - t)(D/E)]$$

Relever of the Beta:

$$\beta^* = \beta_u x [1 + (1 - t)(D/E)^*]$$

= targeted company data

Cost ofcapital equity formula (based on CAPM model):

$$i_e = r_f + \beta(r_m - r_f)$$

rf= risk free
β= Beta
rm= risk premium

To complete the enterprise value analysis is needed to consider the concept of terminal value. The terminal value is based on the final year of the business plan. For instance, if the valuation is run over four years, the terminal value is calculated in year four.

The terminal value equals the cash flow estimated in year n (the last year of the investment, in the example above, year 4) multiplied by one plus g, where g is the growth rate, divided by WACC minus g, and finally divided by one plus WACC to the power n.

The idea of g, the growth rate, is missing. The purpose behind the growth rate is to include in the terminal value the company's expected sales growth in the years after the end of the business plan. It is difficult to define g as it is only based on the forecast. As a result, best practices must be employed. If the expected growth is not aggressive, the ideal strategy is to employ a g range between zero and one. On the contrary, when the forecast of growth is particularly aggressive, a range between one and two must be used.

Terminal value formula:

$$TV_n = \frac{\frac{CF_n \times (1+g)}{(WACC-g)}}{(1 + WACC)^n}$$

g = growth rate

Three more items are required to complete the equity value formula. The first one is the net financial position. It is the difference between the amount of debt and cash that the company owns. The second is called Minorities, even if they are uncommon in private equity, this item indicates the number of shares of the company owned by minority investors, and lastly, the lost surplus assets; in this case, surplus assets are assets held by the firm but do not necessarily generate operating profit for the company.

A Real Case Valuation

Now that the theoretical aspects have been covered, the concept of equity value and the DCF methodology must be applied to a real-world example.

The example will be based on a company called French Winery, which is a French company that is not publicly traded. The company looks like a good candidate for private equity investment. In 2022, the owners of French Winery decide to seek a PE investor to sustain growth and, in the long run, to prepare an acquisition campaign.

The prediction for the next four years is based on the following assumptions from the business strategy, which advisors oversee:

French Winery Profit & Losses statement (EUR € millions)	2022	2023	2024	2025
Sales	49 860	52 756	56 698	61 721
Operating cost	39 379	40 910	43 782	45 714
EBITDA	**10 481**	**11 846**	**12 916**	**16 007**
Depreciation	1 768	2 305	2 305	2 388
EBIT	**8 713**	**9 541**	**10 611**	**13 619**
Interest expenses	300	36	36	36
Taxes	1 648	4 074	4 378	5 710
Net Income	**6 765**	**5 431**	**6 197**	**7 873**

Figure 5: P&L Statement

French Winery Cash Flow statement (EUR € millions)	2022	2023	2024	2025
Depreciation (+)	1 768	2 305	2 305	2 388
Increase net working capital (-)	9 788	4 500	500	500
Capex (-)	3 000	3 975	1 322	500

Figure 6: CF Statement

Comparable companies Beta & Mutiples	Beta	EV/Sales	EV/EBITDA	D/E
Mondavi (US)	0,73	6,20	26	9,45
Beringer (US)	0,94	5,50	22,9	5,25
Southcorp (AUS)	1,02	8,50	24,9	8,25
Bodegas (SP)	0,89	8,50	26,7	8,35
Campari (ITA)	1,23	6,70	24,7	7,35
Antinori (ITA)	not listed	4,90	26,9	7,85
Average	0,962	6,72	25,35	7,75

Figure 7: Comparison Table

French Winery Extra information (EUR € millions)			
Financial data		**Other data**	
Net financial position	10 000	Risk free rate	0.934%
Debt	12 500	*(calculated as five years French Government bonds)	
Equity	8 000	Return on investment	7,75%
PPE	12 000	Holding period (in years)	4
		Growth rate	0,25%
		Corporate taxes	35%

Figure 8: Extra Information

Using the formula computing the equity value is known but determining the company's cash flows is the first challenge. The company's business strategy, four years of profit and loss record, and the profit and loss statement are provided. Based on these documents, the fourth cash flow needed to apply this method can be found. If the four values of cash flows are provided, it is possible to discount them.

To determine the present value and discount them, the WACC needs to be calculated. Both the net cost of debt and the cost of equity to calculate the WACC are required.

As mentioned in the previous chapter calculating the net cost of debt is relatively straightforward. The corporate tax rate set at 35% is provided, and the only difficulty is determining the cost of debt.

The company's balance sheet figures are used to find the amount of interest expenses, which is 300, and the quantity of debt, which is 12,500; these two results are divided, and the result 2.4% represents the cost of debt. Then to calculate the net cost of debt, the cost of debt needs to be multiplied by the tax shield, which gives a net cost of debt result of 1.56 percent.

Calculation of cost of debt net of tax:

$$i_d^* = 300/12,500 * (1 - 0.35)$$

Cost of debt = 300/12,500=2.4%
Net cost of debt= 1.56%

However, the difficulty now is to compute the cost of equity. Some inputs to calculate the cost of equity are needed, which are provided in the documents mentioned earlier.

The inputs required are the risk premium and the risk-free. However, there is an issue with determining the beta. Some comparable companies are needed to calculate the beta. Because the company operates in the wine industry, a list of similar companies that are relevant to the company's valuation has been provided. Thanks to this list, it is feasible to determine the average beta of comparable companies from the list, which is 0.962. But there is still an issue regarding the unlever and relever processes. The debt-to-equity ratio of these companies to run the unlever process is required. If the debt-to-equity ratio of these companies is provided, the unlever beta can be calculated. Once the unlever beta is known, it is feasible to relever it by using the debt-to-equity ratio of French Winery; the result obtained is 0.32.

Beta unlever calculation:

$$\beta_u = 0.962/[1 + (1 - 0.35)(7.75)]$$

The beta Unlever is equal to 0.1593. Once this Beta is calculated, the result can be computed to the Beta relever calculation.

Beta relever calculation:

$$\beta^* = 0.1593374741[1 + (1 - 0.35)(1.56)]$$

The Beta relever is equal to 0.320905. To clarify one, point 1.56 is obtained by calculating the debt-to-equity ratio of French Winery.

This beta value is greater than the beta value of the comparable firms because French Winery's debt-to-equity ratio is lower than the debt-to-equity ratio of the similar companies. It comes as no surprise. Suppose this beta value is taken and applied with the cost of equity calculation (cost of equity equals risk-free rate plus beta multiplied by risk premium minus risk-free). In that case, the cost of equity result is obtained, which is 0.03121 or 3.12 percent.

Cost of equity calculation:

$$i_e = 0.00934 + 0.320905(0.0775 - 0.00934)$$

The net cost of debt and the cost of equity are now known, based on that, calculating the WACC is relatively easy, and the result get of this new calculation is 0,02168 (or 2.17%).

WACC calculation:

$$i_{WACC} = 0.0156 * \frac{12,500}{12,500 + 8,000} + 0.0312 * \frac{8,000}{12,000 + 8,000}$$

The terminal value calculation can now be found. To compute a terminal value, the G rate input is required. French Winery has a G rate of 0.25 percent (this rate suggests that the projection of the company's growth after year four is not highly aggressive). Using this input and the previous results, a terminal value at year four can be calculated.

The inputs are represented by the cash flow in year four by the WACC and the G growth rate of 0.25 percent, with a total terminal value of 445 million euros.

Terminal value calculation:

$$TV_n = \frac{\frac{9,297*(1+0.0025)}{(0.0217-0.0025)}}{(1+0.0217)^4}$$

The 0.0217 is equal to the 2.17% of WACC (calculated the step before) and the 0.0025 is equal to the growth rate of 0,25%

However, the net financial situation must also be considered to arrive at an equity value. To do so, information from the balance sheet will be useful. There are no minorities (which is extremely usual in private equity investment), and in the case of French Winery, some surplus assets are on the balance sheet. When all these items are added together, the equity value of French Winery can be found, and the result is 449.4 million Euros. (To be precise, the equity value is 449,416,032.)

The process used is related to the DCF's valuation, but other types of valuation are possible even if this book does not focus on them.

Equity value calculation:

$$\frac{11,350}{(1+0.0217^4)} + 437,000 + (12,000 - 0 - 10,000)$$

11,350 is equal to the sum of all CF during the four years
0.0217 is the WACC rate
437,000 is the terminal value found just previously
12,000 is the Surplus of Asset mentioned in the extra information
0 is the fact that no minorities are in the company
10,000 is the net financial position

The issue discussed in the previous section of this chapter is that the best practice is to compare the equity value obtained from the DCF with comparable firms in the sector of French Winery. To do so, some multiples are provided; it is important to refer to them as they have been used to compute Beta earlier in the process. Comparable multiples resulting from enterprise value are relevant. Using these multiples, the equity value of French Winery can be determined given the criteria of market transactions.

In this example, two multiples will be employed. The first is the enterprise value divided by sales and the second is the enterprise value divided by EBITDA.

The multiple in the first example is 6.72, whereas the multiple in the second case is 25.23. The enterprise value of French Winery using these two multiples may be computed. In the first situation, the enterprise value may be 334 million euros, whereas it could be 264 million euros in the second case.

It makes sense to calculate an average in both circumstances because it is an enterprise value. It also makes sense to incorporate the net financial position of minorities and the surplus asset of French Winery. Using the multiples, the equity value of French Winery can be determined to be 301 million Euros.

What does this equity value for multiples mean? The meaning is that if the DCF is used, the equity value of French Winery would be greater than the equity value that the market is willing to pay at the time. So, the goal for any private equity investor is to be able to negotiate the proper price because there are two different signals. One indication comes from the DCF, a sort of implicit value of the company, but the market signal is entirely different.

for French Winery Forecast of the enterprise value (EUR € millions)	Ratio	Sales	EBITDA
EV/Sales	6,72	49 860,00	
EV/EBITDA	25,23		10 481,00
EV from EV/Sales		334 893,00	
EV from EV/EBITDA		264 470,57	
Average EV from comparables		**299 681,78**	
(-) Net financial position		10 000,00	
(+) Surplus assets		12 000,00	
(-) Minorities		0,00	
EQUITY VALUE		**301 681,78**	

Figure 9: Forecast of Enterprise Value

Applying Company Valuation with DCF Method

All the tools to determine equity value are now known, from the use of DCF techniques to the use of multiple similar companies.

Everything is ready and needs to be applied to private equity negotiations. As shown in the last part, there is a difficulty with a double valuation in PE transactions because the equity value at time 0 cannot be determined. When the PEI decides to invest, another issue is calculating the equity value at the end (during the exit stage). However, it is crucial to determine both as they will affect the final IRR

There are two options for dealing with the problem of double valuation. The first one will be covered in this part, while the second one will be the topic of the coming part.

The first issue is based on the notion that calculating the equity value at time 0 is not a problem. It is not a concern because the business plan is sound, and the assumptions are reasonable. That suggests the equity value computed with DCF is quite acceptable. It will be an entirely different scenario for startups or circumstances where the business model is insufficient (the second case, explained in the coming part).

For a company in its expansion or replacement phase, it is relatively easy to determine its value based on the business plan, and it is also a common way to do it.

The second issue is a bit more challenging as the exact equity value at time n is unknown and difficult to calculate. Because to calculate the equity value at the time n using the DCF again, another business plan for the years after the end of the one provided will be needed, which is extremely difficult to get. So, to face this issue, calculations are based on the statistics that investors can have in hand.

Now that the theoretical part has been covered, it is time to put these ideas into practice with an example. The investor has the company's business plan in his/her hands, which spans six years, from 2022 to 2027. The equity value at time zero using the DCF approach needs to be calculated and then, based on the first result, the equity value based on multiples at the exit time can be found. This approach is very relevant because an evaluation is needed to see if there is enough flexibility inside the business plan to get a particular IRR that makes sense for the private equity investor in relation to the expected return on the total portfolio now that this has been explained adding some figure will help to clarify this point.

Assume that the PEI's investment is 4.50 million euros and that 4.50 million euros represent 30 percent of the company's equity using DCF. The challenge now is calculating the equity value at the exit, which requires running another assumption, this time linked to the holding duration; in this case, the holding period is three years. That means the business plan must take three years into account: 2022, 2023, and 2024.

A focus must be carried on 2024, the year of leaving, and in this year, two numbers, EBITDA and net financial position need to be identified.

Both numbers are significant as they will directly impact the equity value at the exit. For instance, if the EBITDA in year 3 is 6 million euros and a ratio of 4 is applied, the final value would be 24 million euros. However, if there is 24 million and a net financial position of 4 million, the equity value can be calculated as 24 million minus 4 million. This equates to 20 million euros. The corporation's equity value at the exit is represented by 20 million euros using multiples.

In some ways, the task is done because if the investor holds 30 percent, at the time of the exit, 30 percent of 20 million is six million euros. So, the amount invested is 4.5 million euros at time zero, intending to have 6 million euros in hands after three years.

Inputs from the business plan	
Expected EBITDA at exit	?
Expected holding period	3
Expected NFP at exit	?
Expected EBITDA multiple at the exit	4
PE investment	4 500 000 €
Post monay share percentage	30%

Figure 10: Business Plan Input

Business plan (EUR € millions)						
	Holding period					
	2022	2023	2024	2025	2026	2027
Sales	35 000	39 000	43 000	45 000	50 000	54 000
Operating costs	31 000	33 000	37 000	39 000	43 000	46 500
EBITDA	4 000	6 000	6 000	6 000	7 000	7 500
Depreciation	1 500	1 500	1 500	2 000	2 000	2 000
EBIT	2 500	4 500	4 500	4 000	5 000	5 500
Other Incomes	0	0	0	0	0	0
Interest expenses	120	100	100	75	75	75
EBT	2 380	4 400	4 400	3 925	4 925	5 425
Taxes	816	1 483	1 483	1 308	1 641	1 808
Net Income	1 564	2 917	2 917	2 617	3 284	3 617
Net financial position	4 500	4 000	4 000	3 500	3 500	3 000
Increase in net working capital	1 000	1 000	1 200	1 200	1 200	1 200
Capex	5 000	1 000	1 000	5 000	1 000	1 000
Cash Flow	6 316	483	483	3 808	859	1 692

Figure 11: Business Plan Detailed

If the IRR is calculated for a three-year holding period, the projected IRR is 10.06 percent. The thing is not to determine if 10% is good or bad. It is impossible to justify without comparison, but each PEI, according to his or her expected return, can determine whether it is a decent return or not. However, it is feasible to run a sensitivity analogy, and thanks to it, two separate parameters of the matrix can be combined (see table 12).

On the one hand, the investor can employ the various multiples that he/she can expect. On the other hand, different holding times can be considered. For example, if the previous case, the assumption of the holding period is three years and a multiple of four, by having a look at the matrix, the multiple found is 10,06% of the IRR. But if another simulation is run, the holding period becomes four or five years rather than three. In this situation, the IRR values in the matrix are completely altered.

Another factor is the EBITDA multiple; if this one is boosted, it means that investors are betting on the market's growth. In this situation, the expected IRR will increase.

A straightforward but basic notion. Is that if investors stay, or their holding duration is longer, a bet on bigger multiples must be made to achieve a higher IRR. The game is risky, but it is one of the responsibilities of any PEI to make such a decision.

| | | EBITDA Multiple | | | | | |
		3	4	5	6	7	8
Holding Period	1	-6,67%	33,33%	73,33%	113,33%	153,33%	193,33%
	2	-3,39%	15,47%	31,66%	46,06%	59,16%	71,27%
	3	-2,27%	10,06%	20,12%	28,73%	36,32%	43,15%
	4	-1,71%	7,46%	14,74%	20,86%	26,16%	30,87%
	5	-1,37%	5,92%	11,63%	16,36%	20,43%	24,01%
	6	-1,14%	4,91%	9,60%	13,46%	16,76%	19,64%

Figure 12: Matrix Table

Applying Company Valuation with VCM Method

As seen in the previous part, a first option can be used to manage the issue of double valuation within private equity. However, it is based on the existence of a solid and robust business plan, but some companies, especially startups, cannot provide this requirement. To analyze this type of company, a second option needs to be developed. Any type of venture capital investment uses this option as it allows analysis without a robust business plan. But not only does the startup financing stage take advantage of this method, but the seed financing stage will also be based on this method.

In this scenario, the approach used is the one of duplicate evaluation, which is very different from the first one. While the equity value at time 0 was computed using the DCF in the first case, it is impossible to use the DCF in the second story because, as previously said, the business plan is not strong enough to apply and announce the DCF process. In this instance, the VCM, or venture capital method, must be employed; this method is based on two pillars.

The first is that the investor's IRR is not an outcome of the evaluation but rather one of the inputs, and the second is tied, as in the first scenario, to the amount of money the PEI has to invest. The venture capital method consists of five distinct steps.

The first step is to compute the terminal value. That implies imagining the holding duration for the PEI and then adding the terminal value. In this scenario, the DCF as done in the first case cannot be employed, and multiples need to be used again. The multiple of enterprise value divided by EBITDA is not always used. In most circumstances, the enterprise earnings multiple is the most appropriate manner of applying multiples.

The second stage focused on calculating the future worth of an investment. That means, based on what the PEI is willing to invest, then the future value of the investment is calculated by using, on the one hand, the IRR desired and expected, and on the other, the holding time.

The third stage is based on the percentage of shares related to the data phase. In this scenario, calculating the percentage of shares is quite simple as the future value of the investment must be divided by the terminal value computed earlier using comparable and multiples.

The fourth step involves calculating the number of new shares to issue. In this scenario, the formula needed is the percentage of shares that need to be issued equal to the number of new shares to be issued divided by the number of new shares plus the old one. In this equation, the unknown variable is the number of new shares that must be issued.

The value of newly issued shares represents the final phase, the future value of the investment must be divided by the number of new shares in this case.

These five processes need to be applied to a real-world case. Consider a 4.5 million investment, which is the money required to fund the company. The predicted IRR for the venture capital investment is 45 percent. The other assumptions are related to the holding period, which is, in this situation, five years (this amount of time is sufficient for many seed financing and startup financing deals), then the terminal year net income, which is the variable fundamental to calculate the equity value of the exit, is 3.5 million; the multiple needed is a price-earnings comparable ratio, and in this example, it is 12. Finally, the number of existing shares is 100,000 shares.

Data Inputs	
Value of the investment	4 500 000 €
Expected IRR	45%
Expected holding period	5
Terminal net year income	3 500 000 €
P/E comparable ratio	12
Number of existing shares	100000

Figure 13: Data for VCM

Now that all the data have been provided, the five-step approach must be applied to determine the company's current equity value.

First and foremost, the investment's future value must be calculated. In this situation, it is simply because the investment's worth is known (4.5 million), and this amount needs to be multiplied by one plus 45 percent. to the power of five, where five is the holding time

Future value of the investment:

$$4,500,000 * (1 + 45\%)^5 = 28,843,803.28$$

The second factor is relevant to calculating the terminal amount, and in this situation, 3.5 million must be multiplied by 12. That means the company's terminal value in year 5 is 42 million. Thanks to this calculation, the terminal value is now known and, as consequence the future worth of our investment too.

Terminal value (at the end of the period):

$$3,500,000 * 12 = 42,000,000$$

Based on this second calculation, the percentage of shares for the venture capital investor can be determined, which is, in this case, 68.68 percent. This is an essential step as it is thanks to it that the number of new shares will be computed. And the calculation is based on the shares issued using this percentage and the number of current shares, which is 100,000.

Percentage of share for the VC investor:

$$\frac{28,834,803.28}{42,000,000} = 68.68\%$$

Number of new shares:

$$\frac{100,000 * 68.68\%}{(1 - 68.68\%)} = 219,284.80$$

The last calculation needs to be used as the number of new shares to be issued, and the future value of the investment are known. The price per share can be calculated and, in this case, it is 20.53 euros. The good point is that the number of shares is known thanks to this calculation. Of course, knowing the number of new shares to be issued allows for determining the number of shares remaining after the venture capital investor's investment, which is important for the entrepreneur to continue raising money.

Price per share:

$$\frac{4,500,000}{219,284.80} = 20.52$$

5 Conclusion

The private equity business is a unique realm, which is vital to understand as more and more private equity funds emerge or are open to retailers each year. They play a significant role in the current economy and must no longer be overlooked.

An essential step toward understanding the world of private equity and venture capital has been taken by reading this book. More than just a big picture, more detailed facts about this world have been developed, such as the numerous types of private investors and how to value a company that is not listed on the stock exchange. And how generally this universe functions.

After reading this book, many questions may have been addressed, but you may also have many new ones arising from your reading. If you have any queries, I welcome you to message me on LinkedIn, and I will be happy to answer them.

But I genuinely hope this guide gave you a first idea of the PE & VC world and enough input to approach the PE & VC story from a different perspective.

In any case, I wish you a lot of success either with your startup or with your career in the investment world. I hope that this book could help you to immerse in the private equity topic and that you will use the power of this industry to your advantage.

Killian

6 Reference list

More than 120 articles, books, and videos have helped to write this book. The most essential and meaningful sources are mentioned here. However, some other ones may be forgotten. The APA 7th edition has been used to build this reference list, which means that the sources will not be found as they appear in the book but in alphabetical order.

Admin-economics. (n.d.). *Shadow costs – shadow pricing*. Economics Help. Retrieved June 1, 2022, from https://www.economicshelp.org/blog/glossary/shadow-costs-shadow-pricing/

Agrawal, A. K. (2010, October 29). *The Geography of Crowdfunding*. SSRN. Retrieved June 1, 2022, from https://papers.ssrn.com/sol3/papers.cfm?abstract_id=1692661

AIC. (2022, April 7). *SMEs to benefit from record funding as VCTs raise over a billion in 2021/22 tax year*. The AIC. Retrieved June 1, 2022, from https://www.theaic.co.uk/aic/news/press-releases/smes-to-benefit-from-record-funding-as-vcts-raise-over-a-billion-in-202122

AIFMD. (n.d.). *AIFMD | Invest Europe*. InvestEurope.Eu. Retrieved May 31, 2022, from https://www.investeurope.eu/policy/key-policy-areas/aifmd/

Amundi. (2021, August 6). *Private Debt*. Amundi Institutional. Retrieved June 1, 2022, from https://www.amundi.com/institutional/private-debt

Analysis, K. J.-. (2007, August 9). *Distress investors take private equity cues*. Reuters. Retrieved June 2, 2022, from https://www.reuters.com/article/reutersEdge/idUSN0844208020070809

Attract Capital. (2019, April 30). *Business Finance Consultant*. Retrieved May 31, 2022, from https://www.attractcapital.com/business-expansion-financing.html

A. (2021a, December 15). *Private Equity and Venture Capital Recap (2.2/5) Anglo-Saxon Format*. Medium. Retrieved June 1, 2022, from https://medium.com/@ankur.bpgc/private-equity-and-venture-capital-recap-2-2-5-anglo-saxon-format-8e9bb5366b6b

Balderton. (2022, March 2). *The VC investment decision-making process - Balderton Capital*. Balderton Capital - Series A-Focused European Venture Capital Firm. Retrieved June 2, 2022, from https://www.balderton.com/build/venture-capital-decision-making-process/

BDC. (2021, August 12). *Early-stage investing*. BDC.Ca. Retrieved May 31, 2022, from https://www.bdc.ca/en/articles-tools/entrepreneur-toolkit/templates-business-guides/glossary/early-stage-investing

Bhatt, A. R. (2021, February 24). *Early Stage Funding: Pre-seed, Seed, and Beyond | AbstractOps*. AbstractOps. Retrieved May 31, 2022, from https://www.abstractops.com/blog/early-stage-funding

Blackrock. (n.d.). *Closed End Funds – Investment Guide*. Retrieved June 1, 2022, from https://www.blackrock.com/us/individual/education/closed-end-funds

Brex. (2020, June 15). *What is startup financing and how can you qualify?* Retrieved May 31, 2022, from https://www.brex.com/blog/startup-financing/

California Tax Center. (n.d.). *Limited Partnerships*. CA.Gov. Retrieved June 1, 2022, from https://www.taxes.ca.gov/Income_Tax/limitedpartbus.html

Capital.Com. (2019, July 30). *What is Vulture fund*. Retrieved May 31, 2022, from https://capital.com/vulture-fund-definition

Carta Inc. (2020, June 2). *What is a special purpose vehicle (SPV)?* Carta. Retrieved June 1, 2022, from https://carta.com/blog/special-purpose-vehicle-spv/

Chen, J. (2021, November 11). *What Is a Markdown?* Investopedia. Retrieved June 1, 2022, from https://www.investopedia.com/terms/m/markdown.asp

Chen, J. (2022a, May 17). *What Is a Closed-End Fund?* Investopedia. Retrieved June 1, 2022, from https://www.investopedia.com/terms/c/closed-endinvestment.asp

Chen, J. (2022b, May 27). *Carried Interest Definition*. Investopedia. Retrieved June 1, 2022, from https://www.investopedia.com/terms/c/carriedinterest.asp

Corbey, M. F. D. R. (2019, September 28). *Company life cycle models and business valuation*. MaandbladVoor Accountancy EnBedrijfseconomie. Retrieved May 31, 2022, from https://mab-online.nl/article/37561/

Cornell law school. (n.d.). *Limited partnership*. LII / Legal Information Institute. Retrieved June 1, 2022, from https://www.law.cornell.edu/wex/limited_partnership
Corporate Finance Institute. (2021a, January 29). *Hands-Off Investor*. Retrieved May 31, 2022, from https://corporatefinanceinstitute.com/resources/knowledge/trading-investing/hands-off-investor/

Corporate Finance Institute. (2021b, September 15). *Discounted Cash Flow DCF Formula*. Retrieved June 2, 2022, from https://corporatefinanceinstitute.com/resources/knowledge/valuation/dcf-formula-guide/#:%7E:text=The%20DCF%20formula%20is%20used,investment%20(the%20discount%20rate).

Corporate Finance Institute. (2022a, January 22). *2 and 20 (Hedge Fund Fees)*. Retrieved June 1, 2022, from https://corporatefinanceinstitute.com/resources/knowledge/trading-investing/2-and-20-hedge-fund-fees/

Corporate Finance Institute. (2022b, January 24). *Business Life Cycle*. Retrieved May 31, 2022, from https://corporatefinanceinstitute.com/resources/knowledge/finance/business-life-cycle/

Corporate Finance Institute. (2022c, January 24). *DCF Terminal Value Formula*. Retrieved June 2, 2022, from https://corporatefinanceinstitute.com/resources/knowledge/modeling/dcf-terminal-value-formula/

Corporate Finance Institute. (2022d, January 30). *What is Sensitivity Analysis?* Retrieved June 2, 2022, from https://corporatefinanceinstitute.com/resources/knowledge/modeling/what-is-sensitivity-analysis/

Corporate Finance Institute. (2022e, February 1). *Unlevered Beta / Asset Beta*. Retrieved June 2, 2022, from https://corporatefinanceinstitute.com/resources/knowledge/valuation/unlevered-beta-asset-beta/

Corporate Finance Institute. (2022f, April 28). *Internal Rate of Return (IRR)*. Retrieved June 2, 2022, from https://corporatefinanceinstitute.com/resources/knowledge/finance/internal-rate-return-irr/

Corporate Finance Institute. (2022g, May 7). *IPO Process*. Retrieved June 2, 2022, from https://corporatefinanceinstitute.com/resources/knowledge/finance/ipo-process/

D'angelo financial service. (n.d.). *The Investment Planning and Management Process*. Raymondjames.Com. Retrieved June 2, 2022, from https://www.raymondjames.com/loudangelo/services/our-approach/the-investment-planning-and-management-process

D'Angelo financial service. (n.d.). *The Investment Planning and Management Process*. Raymonjames.Com. Retrieved June 2, 2022, from https://www.raymondjames.com/loudangelo/services/our-approach/the-investment-planning-and-management-process

Deutsche Beteiligungs AG. (n.d.). *THE BENEFITS OF PRIVATE EQUITY*. Dbag.Com. Retrieved May 31, 2022, from https://www.dbag.com/our-business/the-benefits-of-private-equity

Downey, S. (2018, July 6). *Why A VC Passed On Your Startup: The Market-Related Reasons*. Forbes. Retrieved May 31, 2022, from https://www.forbes.com/sites/forbesfinancecouncil/2018/07/06/why-a-vc-passed-on-your-startup-the-market-related-reasons/?sh=5c3e72ab3b18

DWS. (n.d.). *Closed-End Funds | DWS*. Fundus.Dws. Retrieved June 1, 2022, from

By Killian Helf

https://fundsus.dws.com/us/en-us/products/closed-end-funds.html

Elvinger, F. (2020, September 22). *Five Steps to Success: A Private Equity Fundraising Checklist*. Toptal Finance Blog. Retrieved June 2, 2022, from https://www.toptal.com/finance/private-equity-consultants/private-equity-fundraising-checklist

Enterprise Investors. (2021, May 18). *Expansion financing*. Retrieved May 31, 2022, from https://www.ei.com.pl/en/investments/types-of-transactions/expansion-financing/

European Comission. (n.d.-a). *Press corner*. European Commission - European Commission. Retrieved June 1, 2022, from https://ec.europa.eu/commission/presscorner/detail/et/MEMO_15_4609

European Comission. (n.d.-b). *Proposal for a directive on corporate tax transparency*. European Commission - European Commission. Retrieved June 1, 2022, from https://ec.europa.eu/info/publications/proposal-directive-corporate-tax-transparency-country-country-reporting_en

European commission. (n.d.). *Press corner*. European Commission - European Commission. Retrieved June 1, 2022, from https://ec.europa.eu/commission/presscorner/detail/en/IP_22_2884

European Venture Philanthropy Association. (2020, April 1). *What is venture philanthropy?* EVPA. Retrieved June 1, 2022, from https://evpa.eu.com/about-us/what-is-venture-philanthropy

Eversheds Shutherland. (n.d.). *About SBICs*. Publicly Traded Private Equity. Retrieved June 1, 2022, from https://www.publiclytradedprivateequity.com/Structures/About-SBICs

Exupéry, M. C. D. S. (2022, May 17). *The European Venture Capital Funds (EuVECA) and European Social Entrepreneurship Funds (EuSEF) Regulations*. Société Générale. Retrieved May 31, 2022, from https://www.securities-services.societegenerale.com/en/insights/views/news/venture-capital-funds-and-social-entrepreneurship-funds/

Fatica, S. (2013, January). *The Debt-Equity Tax Bias: Consequences and Solutions*. Cairn.info. Retrieved June 1, 2022, from https://www.cairn.info/revue-reflets-et-perspectives-de-la-vie-economique-2013-1-page-5.htm

Faughnder, R. (2021, February 17). *Why Hollywood is obsessed with SPACs*. Los Angeles Times. Retrieved June 1, 2022, from https://www.latimes.com/entertainment-arts/business/newsletter/2021-02-16/hollywood-spacs-beachbody-investments-disney-the-wide-shot

Fernando, J. (2021, December 1). *Initial Public Offering (IPO)*. Investopedia. Retrieved June 2, 2022, from https://www.investopedia.com/terms/i/ipo.asp#:%7E:text=Key%20Takeaways-,An%20initial%20public%20offering%20(IPO)%20refers%20to%20the%20process%20of,S

EC)%20to%20hold%20an%20IPO.

Fernando, J. (2022, February 24). *Internal Rate of Return (IRR)*. Investopedia. Retrieved June 2, 2022, from https://www.investopedia.com/terms/i/irr.asp#:%7E:text=The%20IRR%20rule%20states%20 that,may%20be%20to%20reject%20it.

Fidelity. (n.d.). *What Is A Trust? - Fidelity*. Retrieved June 1, 2022, from https://www.fidelity.com/life-events/estate-planning/trusts

Gaby Hardwicke Solicitors. (2019, March 22). *Share Buybacks – Private Companies*. Retrieved June 2, 2022, from https://www.gabyhardwicke.co.uk/briefing-notes/share-buybacks-private-companies/

Ganti, A. (2021, December 2). *What Is Terminal Value (TV)?* Investopedia. Retrieved June 2, 2022, from https://www.investopedia.com/terms/t/terminalvalue.asp#:%7E:text=Terminal%20value%20i s%20calculated%20by,company%20after%20the%20forecast%20period.&text=Where%3A,f or%20the%20last%20forecast%20period

Gifford, J. (2022, April 28). *SPVs unlock VC investing for the broader public*. Tech.Eu. Retrieved June 1, 2022, from https://tech.eu/2022/04/28/spvs-unlock-vc-investing-for-the-broader-public/#:%7E:text=What%20are%20SPVs%3F,in%20a%20specific%20startup%20deal.

Golding. (n.d.). *Investment Process*. Golding Capital Partners. Retrieved June 2, 2022, from https://www.goldingcapital.com/en/fund-managers/investment-process

Grant, R. (2017, April 20). *Crowdfunding vs. seed funding: All money is not created equal*. VentureBeat. Retrieved May 31, 2022, from https://venturebeat.com/2013/06/24/crowdfunding-vs-seed-funding-all-money-is-not-created-equal/

HAYES, A. (2022, January 17). *How to Calculate Cost of Debt*. Investopedia. Retrieved June 2, 2022, from https://www.investopedia.com/terms/c/costofdebt.asp#:%7E:text=There%20are%20a%20cou ple%20of,after%2Dtax%20cost%20of%20debt.

HM Revenue & Customs. (2017, November 22). *Income Tax: encouraging more high-growth investment through Venture Capital Trusts*. GOV.UK. Retrieved June 1, 2022, from https://www.gov.uk/government/publications/income-tax-encouraging-more-high-growth-investment-through-venture-capital-trusts

Hollow, M. (2014, May 25). *Crowdfunding and Civic Society in Europe: A Profitable Partnership?* Matthew Hollow - Academia.Edu. Retrieved May 31, 2022, from https://www.academia.edu/3415172/Crowdfunding_and_Civic_Society_in_Europe_A_Profit able_Partnership

Hudson, M. (2014). *Funds: Private Equity, Hedge and All Core Structures (The Wiley Finance Series)* (1st ed.). Wiley.

HUNTCLUB. (2021, June 6). *Why Seek Out Venture Capital For Your Startup?* Retrieved May 31, 2022, from https://www.huntclub.com/blog/why-seek-out-venture-capital-for-your-startup

Institutional Limited Partners Association. (2019, August 21). *Write-off*. ILPA. Retrieved June 2, 2022, from https://ilpa.org/glossary/write-off/

James, R. (2022, May 19). *Category: Funds*. Private Equity International. Retrieved June 2, 2022, from https://www.privateequityinternational.com/news-analysis/fundraising/

Jenkins, L. (2022, April 6). *Private Equity: Incentivising management teams in uncertain times*. Alvarez & Marsal | Management Consulting | Professional Services. Retrieved June 1, 2022, from https://www.alvarezandmarsal.com/insights/private-equity-incentivising-management-teams-uncertain-times#:%7E:text=It%20is%20widely%20acknowledged%20that,and%20skin%20in%20the%20game.

Katara, H. (2022, May 23). *Cost of Equity Formula*. WallStreetMojo. Retrieved June 2, 2022, from https://www.wallstreetmojo.com/cost-of-equity-formula/

Kazi, B. M. (2021, February 26). *DCF – Sensitizing for Key Variables*. Financial Edge. Retrieved June 2, 2022, from https://www.fe.training/free-resources/valuation/dcf-sensitizing-for-key-variables/

KENNON, J. (2022, March 21). *How Are Stock Prices Determined?* The Balance. Retrieved May 31, 2022, from https://www.thebalance.com/how-stock-prices-are-determined-358144

Kenton, W. (2021, August 31). *What Is the Cost of Equity?* Investopedia. Retrieved June 2, 2022, from https://www.investopedia.com/terms/c/costofequity.asp#:%7E:text=Using%20the%20capital%20asset%20pricing,%2D1)%20%3D%2010.9%25.

Kirsch, K. (2022, April 12). *Startup Financing: How It Works & How to Get It*. Hubspot. Retrieved May 31, 2022, from https://blog.hubspot.com/sales/startup-financing

Koppel Services. (2017, March 31). *Participation exemption*. Retrieved June 1, 2022, from https://www.koppelservices.com/tax/participation-exemption/

K.Reilly, W. B. (2021, April 16). *The Ins and Outs of a Private Company Share Buyback - Fuse*. Fuse Capital. Retrieved June 2, 2022, from https://www.fuse-capital.com/blog/3-ways-debt-can-be-used-to-finance-a-share-buyback#:%7E:text=A%20buyback%20occurs%20when%20the,among%20public%20and%20private%20investors.%E2%80%9D

Law Inside. (n.d.). *Stock Options Sample Clauses: 27k Samples*. Retrieved June 2, 2022, from https://www.lawinsider.com/clause/stock-options

Law Insider. (n.d.-a). *Callable Securities Sample Clauses*. Retrieved June 2, 2022, from https://www.lawinsider.com/clause/callable-securities

Law Insider. (n.d.-b). *Drag-Along Rights Sample Clauses: 2k Samples*. Retrieved June 2, 2022, from https://www.lawinsider.com/clause/drag-along-rights

Law Insider. (n.d.-c). *Exit Ratchet Charge Definition*. Retrieved June 2, 2022, from https://www.lawinsider.com/dictionary/exit-ratchet-charge

Law Insider. (n.d.-d). *Expansion Financing Definition*. Retrieved May 31, 2022, from https://www.lawinsider.com/dictionary/expansion-financing

Law Insider. (n.d.-e). *Lock-up Covenant Sample Clauses*. Retrieved June 2, 2022, from https://www.lawinsider.com/clause/lock-up-covenant

Law Insider. (n.d.-f). *Options, Warrants and Other Convertible Securities Sample Clauses*. Retrieved June 2, 2022, from https://www.lawinsider.com/clause/options-warrants-and-other-convertible-securities

Law Insider. (n.d.-g). *Permitted Covenant Definition*. Retrieved June 2, 2022, from https://www.lawinsider.com/dictionary/permitted-covenant

Law Insider. (n.d.-h). *Puttable Securities Definition*. Retrieved June 2, 2022, from https://www.lawinsider.com/dictionary/puttable-securities

Law Insider. (n.d.-i). *Replacement Financing Definition*. Retrieved May 31, 2022, from https://www.lawinsider.com/dictionary/replacement-financing#:%7E:text=Replacement%20Financing%20means%20one%20or,not%20including%20the%20Required%20Funding.

Law Insider. (n.d.-j). *Right of First Refusal Definition: 2k Samples*. Retrieved June 2, 2022, from https://www.lawinsider.com/dictionary/right-of-first-refusal

Law Insider. (n.d.-k). *Tag-Along Right Sample Clauses: 760 Samples*. Retrieved June 2, 2022, from https://www.lawinsider.com/clause/tag-along-right

Locke Lord. (n.d.). *SBIC FAQs*. SBIC Law. Retrieved June 1, 2022, from https://www.sbiclaw.com/faqs/

Lotfaliei, B. (2021, January 1). *Leashed Capital Structure of Closed-End Funds*. SSRN. Retrieved June 1, 2022, from https://papers.ssrn.com/sol3/papers.cfm?abstract_id=3970865

Lowe, R. (2022, May 12). *Open-ended funds: The race is on*. Real Assets. Retrieved June 1, 2022, from https://realassets.ipe.com/investment-/open-ended-funds-the-race-is-on/10016284.article

M&A science. (n.d.). *What is Private Equity Deal: Structure, Flow, Process (Guide)*. Dealroom.Net. Retrieved June 2, 2022, from https://dealroom.net/faq/private-equity-deal

Majaski, C. (2021, October 25). *What are the Differences Between Closed-End and Open-End Investments?* Investopedia. Retrieved June 1, 2022, from https://www.investopedia.com/ask/answers/042315/what-are-primary-differences-between-closed-end-investment-and-open-end-investment.asp

Massi, M., Shandal, V., Harris, M., Bellehumeur, K., &Schmundt, W. (2021, February 8). *A Hands-On Role for Institutional Investors in Private Equity*. BCG Global. Retrieved May 31, 2022, from https://www.bcg.com/publications/2018/hands-on-role-institutional-investors-private-equity

Meaning of Input Tax Credit Mechanism in GST. (2019, February 9). How to Export Import. Retrieved June 1, 2022, from https://howtoexportimport.com/Meaning-of-Input-Tax-Credit-Mechanism-in-GST-9088.aspx

Mendoza, C. (2021, September 23). *Shadow capital is here to stay*. Private Equity International. Retrieved June 1, 2022, from https://www.privateequityinternational.com/shadow-capital-is-here-to-stay/

Micheal Page. (n.d.). *Hands-on vs. hands-off management*. Michael Page. Retrieved May 31, 2022, from https://www.michaelpage.ie/advice/management-advice/development-and-retention/hands-vs-hands-management

Mollick, E. R. (2013, June 26). *The Dynamics of Crowdfunding: An Exploratory Study*. SSRN. Retrieved June 1, 2022, from https://papers.ssrn.com/sol3/papers.cfm?abstract_id=2088298

Moore, A. (2018, November 12). *Six benefits of private equity investment*. Corridor Business Journal. Retrieved May 31, 2022, from https://corridorbusiness.com/six-benefits-of-private-equity-investment/

Netherlands Chamber of Commerce, KVK. (2022, April 13). *Seed Business Angel Funds*. Business.Gov.Nl. Retrieved May 31, 2022, from https://business.gov.nl/financing-your-business/funding-and-loans/government-funding/seed-business-angel-funds/

NEWCO. (n.d.). *Participation Exemption | NEWCO - Corporate Services Provider*. Newco.Pro. Retrieved June 1, 2022, from https://www.newco.pro/en/invest-in-portugal/tax-and-accounting-information-in-portugal/participation-exemption

OECD. (n.d.). *Tax Transparency - OECD*. Retrieved June 1, 2022, from https://www.oecd.org/tax/beps/tax-transparency/#:%7E:text=Tax%20transparency%20is%20about%20putting,through%20global%20tax%20co%2Doperation.

Philantropy Impact. (n.d.). *Venture philanthropy | Philanthropy Impact*. Philanthropy-Impact.Org. Retrieved June 1, 2022, from https://www.philanthropy-impact.org/venture-

Private Equity & Venture capital

philanthropy-defining-successful-giving-developing-strategy/venture-philanthropy#:%7E:text=Venture%20philanthropy%20(VP)%20is%20an,year%20support%20and%20capacity%20building

Pitch Book. (2021, July 12). *A guide to every step in the IPO process*. PitchBook. Retrieved June 2, 2022, from https://pitchbook.com/blog/ipo-process-explained
Private Equity Wire. (2022, January 26). *Launches & Fundraising*. Retrieved June 2, 2022, from https://www.privateequitywire.co.uk/category/content-channels/launches-and-fundraising

Rudd, A. (2020, November 2). *What are the four advantages of private equity funds? – nbccomedyplayground*. Nbccomedyplayground. Retrieved May 31, 2022, from https://www.nbccomedyplayground.com/what-are-the-four-advantages-of-private-equity-funds/

Schenk, A. (2015, February 5). *The Tax Credit Mechanism (Chapter 6) - Value Added Tax*. Cambridge Core. Retrieved June 1, 2022, from https://www.cambridge.org/core/books/abs/value-added-tax/tax-credit-mechanism/A7880E0F73C12D9ECAB252840CC3A391

SEC. (2016, December 19). *SEC.gov | Mutual Funds and Exchange-Traded Funds (ETFs) – A Guide for Investors*. SEC.Gov. Retrieved June 1, 2022, from https://www.sec.gov/reportspubs/investor-publications/investorpubsinwsmfhtm.html#factors

SETH, S. (2022, May 23). *What Is the Formula for Weighted Average Cost of Capital (WACC)?* Investopedia. Retrieved June 2, 2022, from https://www.investopedia.com/ask/answers/063014/what-formula-calculating-weighted-average-cost-capital-wacc.asp#:%7E:text=WACC%20is%20calculated%20by%20multiplying,asset%20pricing%20model%20(CAPM).

Sharma, J. K., & Tripathi, S. (2016). *Staged Financing as a Means to Alleviate Risk in VC/PE Financing on JSTOR*. JSTOR. Retrieved June 2, 2022, from https://www.jstor.org/stable/44396794

SPANN, S. (2022, January 9). *Are You a Hands-on or Hands-off Investor?* The Balance. Retrieved May 31, 2022, from https://www.thebalance.com/are-you-hands-on-or-hands-off-investor-4141170

Speiser, M., Bridge, K., LoPreiato-Bergan, M., &Tomczyk, J. (n.d.). *What is an SPV? | AngelList Venture*. LearnAngellist.Com. Retrieved June 1, 2022, from https://learn.angellist.com/articles/spv

SPINK, S. (2007, May). *Distressed Private Equity*. The Hedge Fund Journal. Retrieved June 2, 2022, from https://thehedgefundjournal.com/distressed-private-equity/

Srinivasan, N. (2006). *The Anglo-Saxon Model*. SpringerLink. Retrieved June 1, 2022, from https://link.springer.com/chapter/10.1057/9780230523555_2?noAccess=true&error=cookies_not_supported&code=90640f15-ab50-4acf-b4cd-47147ac274dd

Sumup. (n.d.). *Markdown - What is a markdown? | SumUp Invoices*. SumUp - a Better Way to Get Paid. Retrieved June 1, 2022, from https://sumup.co.uk/invoices/dictionary/markdown/

T. (2021b, November 18). *What Is A Trade Sale In Private Equity? – ictsd.org*. ICSTD. Retrieved June 2, 2022, from https://www.ictsd.org/what-is-a-trade-sale-in-private-equity/#:%7E:text=team%20take%20over.-,What%20Is%20Trade%20Sale%20In%20Private%20Equity%3F,to%20a%20private%20equity%20firm.

TechSlang. (2021, November 19). *What is Seed Funding?*Techslang — Tech Explained in Simple Terms. Retrieved May 31, 2022, from https://www.techslang.com/definition/what-is-seed-funding/

Teijeiro, N., Timmermann, J., & Alicanti, S. P. (2022, April 6). *What is a SPAC? The basics, when you are contemplating going public in 2022*. DLA Piper. Retrieved June 1, 2022, from https://www.dlapiper.com/en/us/insights/publications/2022/04/what-is-a-spac/#:%7E:text=A%20SPAC%20is%20an%20investment,a%20de%2DSPAC%20transaction

Thakur, M. (2021, March 24). *Cost of Debt Formula*. EDUCBA. Retrieved June 2, 2022, from https://www.educba.com/cost-of-debt-formula/

Thakur, M. (2022, May 27). *Vulture Funds*. WallStreetMojo. Retrieved May 31, 2022, from https://www.wallstreetmojo.com/vulture-funds/

The Economist. (2005, December 20). *Anglo-Saxon attitudes*. Retrieved June 1, 2022, from https://www.economist.com/finance-and-economics/2005/12/14/anglo-saxon-attitudes

The Economist. (2007, March 30). *The flat-tax revolution*. Retrieved June 1, 2022, from https://www.economist.com/leaders/2005/04/14/the-flat-tax-revolution

The Law Society. (n.d.). *Trusts*. Retrieved June 1, 2022, from https://www.lawsociety.org.uk/en/public/for-public-visitors/common-legal-issues/trusts

The Startups Team. (2018, December 6). *What Is Startup Funding?* Startups.Com. Retrieved May 31, 2022, from https://www.startups.com/library/expert-advice/what-is-startup-funding

Thune, K. (2022, February 18). *How Stock Prices Are Determined By Transactions*. SeekingAlpha. Retrieved May 31, 2022, from https://seekingalpha.com/article/4452881-how-stock-prices-are-determined

Tillson, M. (2022, March 30). *Private equity or trade sale – what's your best exit?* Grant Thornton UK LLP. Retrieved June 2, 2022, from

Private Equity & Venture capital

https://www.grantthornton.co.uk/insights/private-equity-or-trade-sale-whats-your-best-exit/

Times, T. N. Y. (2004, June 5). *When Private Mixes With Public; A Financing Technique Grows More Popular and Also Raises Concerns*. The New York Times. Retrieved June 1, 2022, from https://www.nytimes.com/2004/06/05/business/when-private-mixes-with-public-financing-technique-grows-more-popular-also.html

TPC. (n.d.). *What is carried interest, and how is it taxed?* Tax Policy Center. Retrieved June 1, 2022, from https://www.taxpolicycenter.org/briefing-book/what-carried-interest-and-how-it-taxed

US Legal, Inc. (n.d.). *Growth Capital Law and Legal Definition | USLegal, Inc.* USlegal.Com. Retrieved June 1, 2022, from https://definitions.uslegal.com/g/growth-capital/

USPEC. (2019, November 5). *Winning Strategy for Better Investment Decisions in Private Equity*. https://www.uspec.org/blog/winning-strategy-for-better-investment-decisions-in-private-equity

Vaidya, D. C. (2022a, June 1). *Fund Management*. WallStreetMojo. Retrieved June 2, 2022, from https://www.wallstreetmojo.com/fund-management/

Vaidya, D. C. (2022b, June 1). *Limited Partners (LP) vs General Partners (GP) in Private equity*. WallStreetMojo. Retrieved June 1, 2022, from https://www.wallstreetmojo.com/limited-partners-lp-vs-general-partners-gp/

Venture Valuation. (n.d.). *Valuation methods | Venture Valuation*. Retrieved June 2, 2022, from https://www.venturevaluation.com/en/methodology/valuation-methods#:%7E:text=Method%3A%20The%20venture%20capital%20method,the%20risk%20the%20investors%20takes.

Volta Venture. (2021, November 25). *Early stage venture capital: everything you should know about*. Retrieved May 31, 2022, from https://www.volta.ventures/early-stage-venture-capital-everything-you-should-know-about/

Wall Street Prep. (2022a, March 30). *Levered and Unlevered Beta: Unsystematic vs Systematic Risk*. Retrieved June 2, 2022, from https://www.wallstreetprep.com/knowledge/beta-levered-unlevered/#:%7E:text=To%20calculate%20unlevered%20beta%2C%20the,company's%20debt%2Fequity%20ratio%5D.

Wall Street Prep. (2022b, April 9). *VC Valuation Method: Valuing Early-Stage Start-Ups (Excel Template)*. Retrieved June 2, 2022, from https://www.wallstreetprep.com/knowledge/vc-valuation-6-steps-to-valuing-early-stage-firms-excel-template/

Wealth Club. (n.d.). *VCT Tax Relief Guide: Income tax relief, tax-free dividends. . . .* Retrieved June 1, 2022, from https://www.wealthclub.co.uk/vct-tax-relief/
Weissmann, A. (2021, April 12). *How does the venture capital method value a*

*business?*Venionaire Capital. Retrieved June 2, 2022, from
https://www.venionaire.com/venture-capital-method/

Young, J. (2022, March 14). *Special Purpose Acquisition Company (SPAC)*.
Investopedia. Retrieved June 1, 2022, from https://www.investopedia.com/terms/s/spac.asp

Young, R. (2020, May 18). *What is a Private Debt Fund?* AB Capital. Retrieved June 1,
2022, from https://trustabcapital.com/what-is-a-private-debt-fund/#:%7E:text=A%20private%20debt%20fund%20specializes,a%20wide%20range%20of%20companies.